My [illegible]
Through Cancer

A Journal of Hope and Healing

By

Martha Sue Wood Bass

Valdese, North Carolina

My Journey Through Cancer: A Journal of Hope and Healing

Editing by Margaret Lue Wood Lackey
Editing and Proofing by Jeffery Wayne Bass
Proofing and Formatting by Allen King
Cover Design by Heather Ward
Published by OutFlow Publishing
Valdese, North Carolina 28690
www.outflowpublishing.com

ISBN-13: 978-1-7329995-6-5

Printed in the United States of America.

Acknowledgements

Thank you

David Anthony Bass, Sr.
(My soulmate for life, my rock and anchor
during this journey)
For asking me to be your wife 53 years ago.
You have kept every vow we pledged, especially
"to love and to cherish in sickness and in health."

Jeffery Wayne Bass
(My middle child, first twin)
For the time you took to proofread and edit
this manuscript and write the Introduction.
Your valuable feedback helped me accomplish
my dream to write my story.

Margaret Lue Wood Lackey
(Wombmate, twin, friend and co-pilot on this endeavor)
For the countless hours you spent typing,
editing and helping select photos.
Most importantly, for encouraging me to do this.
You said, "If I can write my autobiography,
you can write your story."
We did it, Sis!

Dr. Ronald Caldwell
(My trusted physician for many years)
For referring me to Hope Cancer Center and
for every prayer you prayed with me
at every office visit over the years.

Medical Staff and Counsellors
Hope Cancer Center, Asheville North Carolina,
For your sincere compassionate care during chemotherapy,
surgery, difficult days and postoperative follow-up.

Former Pastors, Pastor George Davis and
Members of Emma United Methodist Church
For your love, prayers and being there for me
during the darkest chapter of my life.

Family and Friends
For food, cards, Emails, calls, prayers, love and support
that came just when I needed them most.

God
For your comfort, strength, peace and healing
every step of the way.
I am cancer-free!

Endorsements

At one point, Martha likens her journey to a roller-coaster ride, one that could be aptly named "The Red Devil." We hold our breath and hang on tightly as she plunges downward, losing many to the "C" word along the way. Our hearts scream with her as she races through the loops and twists through the curves; we cheer her on as she emerges from tunnels and climbs to great heights, her eyes fixed on the One in charge of the controls. Collectively, we exhale a sigh of relief as she steps off the ride onto the platform, arms raised in praise, "Cancer-free!"

Katrinia Bass
B.A., Literature,
UNC, Asheville

Lots of memories here, of fear and pain, but much more of deep love and determination between us all. And of all the many people that loved us and inspired us and gave us hope through Mom's journey... Mom did the most. She is the most tender person I've ever met, but what a fighter.

Alan Layne Bass
B.S., Mathematics,
M.S., Mathematics,
UNC, Wilmington
Author, Wiley Publishers

Beautifully written story. Martha promotes courage, faith, love and strength while writing her journey of survival. Inspiring story of winning the battle against the evil of cancer.

Sabrina Dobbins
Certified Medical Assistant (CMA)
Advent Health,
Hendersonville, NC

When John Piper said, “Don’t waste your cancer,” he could’ve had Martha Bass in mind. She and I worked together 13 years at the Cove so I had the privilege of seeing her on her best days but also on some of her hardest. She tells her story in journal form with humor, grit and deep faith, but no “rose colored glasses.” You may not be facing the giant of cancer; but we ALL face giants of one kind or another in our lives. I hope you will be uplifted and challenged as much as I was by reading her story. She doesn’t claim to slay giants; but she points you to the Savior who does. And in so doing, she makes sure that not one iota of her cancer is wasted. I highly recommend Martha’s book about her journey.

Deanna Sales
Dining Room Supervisor/Coordinator, The Cove
Billy Graham Training Center,
Asheville, NC

Although she is short in stature, Martha stands tall in her faith in our Lord Jesus Christ. During this time of her journey, I had the honor and privilege of serving as her Pastor at Emma United Methodist Church. From the very beginning of our time with this wonderful congregation, my wife, Billie, and I knew that Martha was a woman of prayer as she loved and encouraged us. As you read her story of faith in the midst of a dark trial, you too will see this and be inspired to also trust in "The One who holds tomorrow." That is true for all of us as we live in the promise of Philippians 1:6.

George M. Davis
Retired Pastor,
United Methodist Church

In her battle with cancer, my mother chose an attitude of never giving up and to move forward in search of moments of joy amidst suffering and bouts of hopelessness. These pages share her odyssey and the choices she made to help her through. Whatever situation brings you to pick up this book, may her words offer peace in the assurance that you are not alone. And may you also find moments, *"...to make your heart smile."*

David A. Bass, Jr.
B.S., Computer Science,
UNC, Asheville

What an awesome God we have... He heals... Splendid story of a journey of faith

Ronald Caldwell
MD, Advent Health,
Hendersonville, NC

My Journey Through Cancer

A Journal of Hope and Healing

Contents

Introduction.....i

Forward...........iii

Chapters

1 What Is This?- 1
2 Delightful Diversions- 9
3 Return To Reality- 17
4 Facing the "Red Devil" - 31
5 Sensible Surgery- 49
6 The Road to Recovery- 55
7 In the Chair Again -69
8 Faith, Fun, Friends and Family- - - - - - - - - - - - - - - 77
9 What Is Next?- 89
10 Celebrating Survival and Fifty Golden Years- - - 99
11 Meditation: The Significance of Eight- - - - - - - 105
Epilogue- 111

Introduction

If you ever meet my mom, you'll know her immediately. You'll never see anyone who looks so friendly. She is a tiny woman with a giant heart and a bright smile. She stands under five feet tall, with a soft, gentle voice. But if you don't look close or long enough at her, you will never know that there is a true warrior standing before you.

You see, from the time I became a married man, I saw my mother as someone that I needed to secure and protect. I did this through frequent telephone calls, letters, words of affection and a listening ear. But I didn't think of my mom as a warrior. Despite all I'd seen her do – all the work and care she put into raising three boys – I always thought of her as a delicate treasure that needed to be tended and guarded.

That vision of my mom changed in January of 2017, when her cancer diagnosis came. And not just any cancer, a very aggressive form. In this book, you'll read about the day we got the news and the emotional journey that came after. It's a journey full of highs and lows, good news and bad, clarity and confusion, moments to be celebrated, moments to weep, and moments when all we could do was wait and wish for the best.

In the end, it is a journey of hope and healing.

Maybe you are reading this now because you yourself are making that journey. Maybe you know someone who has been or will be. Maybe you need hope and healing yourself or want to help give it to someone else. Whatever brings you to this story I know that within these pages you will find a kind, strong soul whose words and meditations will bring comfort, laughter and warmth. The most harrowing experiences of life are the ones that both shape and reveal who we really are.

This journey we took, and are still taking, has shown me who my mother really is: An inspiration, a blessing, a warrior.

J. Wayne Bass
B.A., English, UNC, Wilmington
M.A., Religious Studies, UT, Knoxville
P.H.D., Asian Languages and Cultures, UCLA
Professor of Humanities, Heartland Community College, Bloomington, IL

Foreword

It is my honor to write the forward for this book. Martha shares in detail her cancer journey. This amazing woman is my wombmate. From the day we entered this world as identical twins, ours was a special relationship. We looked so much alike, it was difficult for Mother and Dad to tell us apart. She would put a pair of pink socks on one and a blue pair on the other. We would exchange and each would wear a blue one and a pink one. That's how much we loved being twins – how much we loved being alike. To this day when we are together, we dress alike just for the fun of it.

When we married and went in separate directions, we changed to become our own person. Martha is known as the country girl; I am the city girl. She enjoys gathering wood to burn in a real fireplace; I prefer to flip a switch for a gas flame. She could live where the Engles did at the *Little House on the Prairie* and go into town once a month for supplies. I would need to live at Olsen's Store because I would have to shop often. Those who know us enjoy these stories and smile.

Martha has gracefully broached the aging process. Her natural gray/white hair is beautiful. I still hang back, fight the progression with low lights, flat/curling irons and anti-aging creams, striving to be forever young.

Despite changes in appearance, we have never lost the close bond we share as twins. When I learned that my twin had cancer, there are no words to describe the pain I felt. I wished I could take her diagnosis. During her journey, from ESP (extra-sensory perception) we have, I knew when she was having a rough day. Once in excruciating pain, I called my massage therapist. When I described my unexplained aching, she said I was trying to carry Martha's pain but reminded me that I didn't need to, Jesus had done that.

This book is written with openness and honesty. Journaled in detail, it winds through trails of disappointment, agony, fear, even desperation. Those off-the-track moments were short lived. Martha refused to linger there. As hope rose within her, she grabbed unto a rope of faith, strength or courage, determined to win this race with victory.

Her theme song, *I Know Who Holds Tomorrow,* rings throughout the book. It enabled her to jump hurdles, refuse to give up and keep going though dark valleys that led to mountain peaks. I will omit details. I want you to read them and be encouraged by her words and bravery.

Her desire is that her story will inspire others (forced to take a cancer journey or one of great adversity) to take one day at a time and know that with God as their pilot, they can make it. Those who have been blessed not to take such a journey will be inspired by her will to live life to its fullest.

Margaret Lue Wood Lackey
A.A., General Studies, East Coast Bible College
B.A., Christian Education, East Coast Bible College
Continuing Education, Lee University

1

What Is This?

Why had it become so uncomfortable to lay on my right side if my breast touched the mattress? I can still see the Christmas cards that lined the chair railing down the hall where I was standing when I did something I had failed to do regularly. I did a self-breast exam.

Oh, God, no, please! I felt a lump in my right breast and immediately started beating myself up because I had missed my mammogram in 2015. Since I was out of town, I had called to cancel my annual appointment and failed to reschedule. Every year following a mammogram, I had received a letter stating that everything looked fine; there were no problems.

I walked outside where my husband David was working on a project and asked him to come inside so we could talk. I explained that I felt something but it could be my imagination.

My soulmate checked and said, “No, Honey, it’s not your imagination. I can feel it, too.” As he held me, the silence screaming from the walls was deafening.

Alan, one of our twin sons, walked into the room and we told him we had discovered something that could be a problem. As he joined our hug, the concern on his pale face was crushing.

I was considered to be in good health at 70 years old and knew of no history of breast cancer in my family. The three of us agreed that the lump could be a fibroid tumor or something minor with nothing to worry about... Despite our positive approach, the "C" word kept creeping into my mind.

December 22, 2016: It was three days until Christmas. We were in Southport, North Carolina, our beach haven, waiting for our Knoxville family to arrive on the 26th.

The house was festive with three large trees, in addition to smaller Christmas trees of all shapes and sizes I had collected through the years. Evergreen garland laid on shelves in the den; a nativity was displayed in our dining room; bells hung throughout the house; and Christmas angels graced every room.

I phoned my doctor's office in Asheville, explained my situation and asked for the first available appointment in January. The physician's assistant encouraged me to try to enjoy the holidays and said the lump could be a number of different things – not necessarily cancer.

Being a twin is such a blessing in my life. Margaret, my wombmate, is also my best friend. When I called her, she was concerned, assured me of her thoughts and prayers and was so supportive. I could feel the strength of her love when she and her husband Ron arrived for their Christmas visit.

My brother Doyle and his wife Judy also joined us for a Southport Christmas celebration. Before they left to go home to Fayetteville, I said, "There's something I need to tell you."

They joined Margaret and me in the bedroom. I shared my apprehensions and asked for their prayers that results of my discovery would be something minor.

Martha, Margaret and Doyle

December 25, 2016: As our precious grandson Drake discovered an array of gifts on Christmas morning, I put my turmoil on hold and smiled throughout the day. But I had to keep reminding myself to breathe.

During our priceless holiday time with our Knoxville family, I wore my happy-face mask. Just before our son, his wife and our three grands, Grace, John and Luke left, I informed DJ and Jamie of the lump and asked them to join those already committed to pray for good results.

January 1, 2017: On our return to Asheville, David and I stopped in Concord, had dinner and spent the night with Margaret and Ron. Margaret's daughter, my niece Christy, and her family dropped by for a visit, assuring me of their prayers in the days ahead.

January 3, 2017: I have been seeing Dr. Ronald Caldwell (my hypertension/primary physician) for a number of years. I only wish anyone who needed a doctor could have one as caring and compassionate as he is. When he examined me, he asked his assistant to phone Hope Cancer Center and make an appointment for me that afternoon. Hope Cancer Center has been treating cancer patients since 1992.

The compassionate doctor and his staff assured me they would "wear Jesus out" praying for me and would check on me regularly.

As I sat at Hope Cancer Center completing page after page of paperwork, I kept thinking this had to be a nightmare. I was going to wake up soon. David sat beside me, assuring me we were in this together and that no matter what the outcome, he would be there for me. His comforting words kept me breathing.

The technicians performed exams and an ultrasound with professionalism while at the same time exhibiting compassion as though I were one of their own. They assured me that my wellbeing was their greatest concern. The radiologist gave no answers to questions screaming in our heads. She said we would learn more when we met with the surgeon once the biopsy scheduled for January 9 was done.

Dr. Blair Harkness came highly recommended as one of the best who had been with Hope Cancer Center since 2006. Learning that he was a preacher's son and the father of twin daughters gave me an immediate connection since I am a preacher's kid and the mother of twins.

January 6, 2017: Snow started to fall in our little mountain town of Asheville, North Carolina. Fluffy white flakes painted a postcard picture for us to view from the huge windows in our Deltec round house. Trees glistened above the pure white blanket beneath them. By Saturday, eight inches of snow had fallen. Watching snow fall as I sat beside a warm cozy fire usually made me feel happy. But today this familiar scene looked different to me. In my state of near panic, the beauty had lost its luster. As I prayed for sleep to come, a hundred scenarios played out in my head. With roads covered in ice beneath the snow, I declared we would never be able to get out of our driveway, much less make it to my scheduled biopsy.

We had airline reservations for Tuesday, January 10, to fly to San Diego for a visit with our son Wayne and his wife, Ashley. Two months earlier, I had made the reservations to fly out of Wilmington, having no idea we would be in Asheville for a biopsy appointment.

My head kept telling me the doctor was going to find a large cancer that needed to be removed immediately. We would not be flying anywhere. Videos the enemy kept playing in my mind were not pleasant to watch; but I could not drown out the sound or delete them. They played over and over.

Snow Fall, Asheville, NC

Thankfully, by Monday the roads had been cleared. The snow had stopped falling; and with the aid of our four-wheel-drive truck, we made it to Hope Cancer Center with no problem. We were packed and ready to head to Southport following my appointment if the doctor would allow us to make the scheduled trip.

Before I had the biopsy, Dr. Harkness went over the results of my mammogram and ultrasound. He asked if the radiologist had told us anything. We responded that she said we would learn more after talking with him, getting the results of the biopsy. Images of the mammogram were disturbing.

The bilateral diagnostic mammogram demonstrated a 5 cm mass in my right breast. Clustered heterogenous calcifications (calcium deposits) looked like white snowflakes floating inside my breast. The kind doctor continued, "I can't be sure until I see the biopsy; but from what I see, I believe the lump in your breast is cancer."

I took David by the hand. And with a look of what I am sure was fear in living color, I muttered, "He just said he believes I have cancer."

David and I told Dr. Harkness that we had reservations to fly to San Diego the following afternoon and asked his advice about what to do. He told us to take the trip and enjoy time with our family.

The biopsy would be back in two days. Brenda, his nurse, would phone us with the results or we could wait to go over them with him when we returned for my appointment on January 18. David and I wanted to hear the results as soon as they came in.

Having never had a breast biopsy before, I had no idea what to expect. First of all, blue dye was rubbed all over the area to be examined. A needle was inserted into my right breast. Then a larger needle, a vacuum-powered probe – was inserted to remove several samples of tissue to be sent to the lab for analysis. A better description of the probe, as seen through my eyes, would be a large Phillip's screwdriver. When Dr. Harkness warned me that he was going to go a little deeper, he was not kidding. But I did not scream, I surprised myself and him and smiled.

Following the procedure, my chest was bandaged. I was given instructions on how to care for the site, permitted to remove the bandage after 24 hours and shower. I had to leave the steri-strips in place for three days. I was told I may have swelling and bruising. Thankfully, I did not experience that.

Despite the fact that I was somewhat uncomfortable following the biopsy, David and I made the six-hour trip to Southport with no problem. With as much enthusiasm as we could exhibit, we packed our bags Monday night and were ready for Alan to drive us to the airport in Wilmington Tuesday afternoon.

Our sweet four-year-old (youngest) grandson, Drake, wanted to help carry our luggage to the terminal and was excited that we were going to get on a big airplane to go see "Unka Wayne and Aunt Ashwe."

Later you will be thrilled to learn about a new grandchild that comes into our life. In our world, those children bring new meaning to the word "grand."

Our first flight went smoothly; and our stopover in Atlanta allowed time for a meal before our flight to San Diego. During the meal, I struggled with my mind as it played images of devastating things that could be ahead for me. Oh, how I wish my mind would stop tormenting me.

The big question, **"What is this?"** continued to torture me as well. It screamed in my head. With hope against all hope, I prayed that what seemed likely was not true. But it was becoming more apparent every day what this lump is – it's cancer.

Drake pulling our luggage at the airport

2

Delightful Diversions

This trip to sunny San Diego, California was a delightful diversion, a great way to help get my mind off the "discovery." The flight from Atlanta was uneventful with an on-time arrival. Wayne and Ashley were waiting for us at the airport. From the onset, they assured us that no matter what we faced in the next few days, we would face it together. We were covered with their support, love and prayers. The Spanish style house they had recently moved into was lovely. Our guest room was well prepared, inviting and welcoming.

We slipped into the comfortable bed beneath fresh, clean sheets, ready for a good night's rest. But our minds were on overload. I kept quoting the scripture I had committed to memory, reminding myself it was written for me:

Jeremiah 29:11: *For I know the thoughts that I think toward you, says the LORD, thoughts of peace and not of evil, to give you a future and a hope.* (NKJV)

January 11, 2017: Wayne, Ashley, David and I rode up to Santa Barbara. We were surrounded by beauty: purple mountain majesty on the right, the multi-colored blue, green and gray ocean on our left with a Carolina blue sky above us.

Ashley had spent hours planning this trip for us (having no idea that during this time I could be facing devastating news). On our first stop, we enjoyed one of the best bagels we had ever eaten. Despite the awesome surroundings, my mind kept listening for my phone to ring. We saw many sites of interest as we passed through Los Angeles, "buying me some time" while waiting for results that could change my life forever.

When we arrived at the Santa Barbara pier, we walked around, admiring the breath-taking view of God's creation. Then we toured the Museum of Natural History Sea Center. This aquatic exploration center offers much to explore with live-touch shark pools, a tide pool tank and magnified sea specimens. I was admiring a magnificent exhibit of star fish when my phone rang. Pausing to remind myself to breathe, I answered it.

"Mrs. Bass, I have the results from your biopsy. Is this a convenient time to talk?"

I explained that we were in the middle of a tour. She said she would call back first thing in the morning. I told her that would be best but I had just one question: "Do I have cancer?"

With compassion in her kind voice, Brenda reluctantly responded, "Yes, Mrs. Bass, you do; and it's bad."

My world stopped on its axis and my body went numb, in a state of shock. I slipped on my mask for my family. What they saw was a strong, brave woman filled with courage and hope. But inside, this little woman was pleading for God to help me breathe.

What I was seeing was memories of funerals I had attended, saying good-bye to people I loved. My sister-in-law, Ann, who died of breast cancer, would not be a part of her son or daughter's wedding. She would not have the privilege of holding her grandchildren. She died at the age of 43.

My sister-in-law Florence died of brain cancer on September 26, 1999. On October 1, just five days later, her first grandchild was born. She never got to hold little William or look into the face of the precious baby she had counted down the days to meet.

My cousin Brenda lived to see her daughter's wedding but died a few months later of stomach cancer. She would never see her grandchildren, either.

I was asking myself, "How would my story end?" Would this diagnosis be the shovel that would dig my grave?"

When we left the museum, we shopped in the little quaint town. Much of my time was spent on the phone with family and friends, updating them as I had promised to do, asking for prayer.

David, Wayne and Ashley, kept some distance. Sensing my pain and stress, they gave me some space and allowed me to privately "do my thing."

I went through the motions of eating at Santa Barbara Brewing Company as my mind silently shouted questions, "What did Brenda mean when she said it was bad? Why did she say that?"

Santa Barbara, CA Area

Ashley had rented an adorable Airbnb near downtown. In that home away from home where we settled in for the night, we ate popcorn and relaxed as we watched a movie, "Love Actually." As I lay quietly in bed, a hundred scenarios played out in my mind, like what would Brenda tell me the following morning. David held me in his arms through the night, stilling my trembling heart as I drifted in and out of sleep.

January 12, 2017: True to her word, Brenda phoned early Thursday morning. My phone was on speaker so David, Wayne and Ashley could hear our conversation. "Mrs. Bass, you have carcinosarcoma metaplastic carcinoma. It is a rare form of cancer found in less than one percent of breast cancer cases." In order to replay what she had said, following Brenda's call, I went to Google on my phone to find answers and read:

> Because it is so rare, few studies of this condition have been done. This cancer has multiple subtypes making it even more difficult. Finding a study that will give you any definitive answers as to why/how you got carcinosarcoma metaplastic carcinoma or what you can do to cure it is impossible. Rare does not mean a death sentence but it is a very scary diagnosis. This type cancer does come back often and quickly. Fifty percent of patients will have a second tumor.

One answer to my many questions had become very clear. I knew why Brenda had said to me on the phone, "It is bad."

From that point on, I made a decision not to do any more research on my diagnosis. I had cancer and it was bad, the most devastating news of my life. That was more than enough to know. There was nothing I could do about it at the moment.

I was in the midst of the most magnificent scenery I had ever seen. The most amazing family in the world was sharing this beauty with me. So I chose to take one day at a time, refusing to allow myself to miss the opportunity of a lifetime.

I would savor the moments of our California visit and remind myself that God, who had painted these awesome scenes for me, was also in control of my life.

We met my nephew Reed, his wife, Jennifer, and their son, Sawyer, for lunch. This sweet little guy, my twin sister's grandson, calls me "Other Grammy." Seeing them was a special treat. Going through the motions of eating with them at the Cheesecake Factory, I played my role of "having it all together" well. I was quickly becoming a seasoned actress.

Thursday evening was so enjoyable. We found several familiar names as we made our way through the Hollywood Walk of Fame. It comprises more than 2,600 five-pointed terrazzo and brass stars with names of famous people embedded in the sidewalks along fifteen blocks of Hollywood Boulevard and three blocks on Vine Street.

Through drizzling rain, we went to Griffith Observatory in Los Angeles and enjoyed the night lights of Hollywood and Los Angeles. As we made this beautiful walk, I thought of my "city girl" sister and wished she were with us.

January 13, 2017: In the early morning hours, we arrived back at Wayne and Ashley's with hearts full of unforgettable memories. I woke several times during the night to find David praying for me.

When we got up, he and I took a relaxing walk. On our return, we found a lovely bouquet of flowers Ashley had placed in our room – a sweet smelling fragrance, a caring thoughtful act of kindness from our special daughter-in-love. Later that day we went to Horton Plaza and Seaport Village, some of our favorite San Diego spots. We dined at Anthony's, one of our favorite restaurants on the bay. That night we relaxed as we watched another good movie and spent time chatting about our favorite things.

January 14, 2017: We walked to one of Wayne and Ashley's favorite diners where they treated us to a delicious breakfast. Then we went to another of my favorite places: Point Loma, a rugged peninsula famous for Cabrillo National Monument and a seaside community within the city of San Diego.

As I gazed in awe at the old Point Loma Lighthouse, enamored by its history and beauty, its beam whispered peace to me. Its brilliant ray was one of hope, reminding me that everything was going to be alright.

Point Loma Lighthouse, San Diego, CA
(My ray of hope)

Saturday evening we met Vince and Lisa, dear friends of Alan, Wayne and Ashley and enjoyed a meal with them. Lisa was such an inspiration to me as she had taken the "cancer journey" before me. Her breast cancer had been diagnosed in January 2016, one year before mine. After all her treatments, one year later, she had been declared cancer free. As she gave me a big assuring hug, she said, "Martha, one day you will get the news I just did. You, too, will be cancer free!"

Through this journey, I discovered that one of the strongest allies a woman can have is another woman who has been through a similar situation. Knowing you have someone on your side is refreshing.

My new friend also gave me a book, *Bald is Better with Earrings*, a survivor's guide to getting through breast cancer. This true account of Andrea Hutton's cancer journey was so helpful. Ironically, this author is from Santa Barbara, the beautiful town I had just been privileged to visit. Her story was similar to mine. She had found a lump in her breast unexpectedly just as I had. And she was shocked at her discovery just as I was.

Sadly within a few months after our visit to San Diego, my friend Lisa got a devastating diagnosis. Her cancer had metastasized to her brain and spinal column. Even while this warrior battled her second round of cancer, she sent me cards, texts and called just to check on me. I reached out to her as well. Across the miles, we stayed in touch. On January 11, 2018 she lost her battle at age 52. This precious lady lives on – not only in my heart but also in the hearts of her soulmate, Vince, her family, friends and many whose lives she touched as an outstanding high school AP English teacher. My life was not only made better for having known this "angel on assignment," it was changed. I will never be the same just for the privilege of having known Lisa Smith.

January 15, 2017: Sunday morning I made chili and sweet tea for a cookout with Ashley's family. Our kids treated us to home-made biscuits and gravy and a new kind of bacon they had found at a near-by farmers' market. What a special time we enjoyed with these new friends. These dear people, Ashley's family, showed me so much love, assuring me of their support and prayers as I began this frightening journey. Just being in their presence brought strength and comfort to my trembling heart.

January 16, 2017: After treating us to another delightful breakfast at another of their favorite places, Wayne took us to the airport for our flight back home. Ashley gave us hugs and a teary good-bye as she left for work.

We arrived at the airport with time to spare before our departure; however, there was a problem in security and our flight kept getting delayed due to the lack of available attendants for this particular flight. Added to the heaviness my heart was feeling from the knowledge of my diagnosis and the pain of having to leave our dear family behind, my anxiety escalated as I feared we would miss our connecting flight from Atlanta to Wilmington. We were 2300 miles from home; and I needed to see my doctor immediately!

My mind, on overload with so many mixed emotions, continued to play cruel and unnecessary tricks on me. Finally, we boarded; and by running to our connecting flight in Atlanta, we barely made it in time. David and I were the last passengers to board the plane. Alan was waiting at the Wilmington airport to take us to Southport.

Wayne, Ashley, Martha and David

San Diego Bay

January 17, 2017: As we left Southport Tuesday, Alan assured us of his love and prayers. The pain on his face made me hurt for him. But at the same time, his love and compassion were reassuring.

We stopped by Margaret and Ron's in Concord on our way to Asheville. Not only did that short visit help to break up the long trip, it boosted my spirits. Our bond of twinship is amazing. Margaret knew when I was having a bad day; and she was trying to carry my pain. She felt that if she could share it, perhaps it would lighten my load. That's what her massage therapist told her when one day, in so much pain, she called her for an emergency appointment.

Again, my niece Christy and her family came by to see us and assure us of their continued love, emotional support and prayers. On that short visit, we shared food, love, laughter, tears and prayers.

The love I saw on the faces surrounding me assured me that I was not taking this journey alone. I was not the only one asking questions. Though no one spoke of them openly, I knew there were many silent questions we all were asking about the journey ahead. But we would face them together. As I took the next step, people I loved would be following close behind me to pick me up if I fell.

As David and I rode toward Asheville, I closed my eyes and laid my head back on the car seat, reliving sweet memories of the amazing journey we had just made to California. The visit we had longed for, talked and dreamed about for months was over. The devastating diagnosis I had gotten while we were there brought on moments of anxiety. But the time we had spent with our kids and the things they had done to make the trip extra special were more than **delightful diversions**.

I had put on my happy-face mask and tried to appear calm. In wearisome moments, when the mask slipped a bit, David, Wayne and Ashley, who had been watching closely, noticed.

The journey (not to California but the road called cancer) had begun. My precious family not only diverted my attention to happy thoughts, they kept me from falling.

3

Return to Reality

January 18, 2017: On our way to my appointment with Dr. Harkness, a friend and former pastor, Rev. David Warren, met us at church to pray with us. His genuine love, concern and encouraging prayer were uplifting and faith-building. As we knelt at the altar, David and I prayed for strength, courage and hope as we made our ghastly entrance into the unknown.

Dr. Harkness went over the biopsy results in detail, explaining that the cancer was estrogen negative, progestion negative and HER2 negative – in short, triple negative breast cancer which can be more aggressive, more difficult to treat, more likely to recur. Carcinosarcoma metaplastic carcinoma is usually approached with treatments prescribed for triple negative breast cancer.

This was not the report we had hoped for, not the one we had prayed not to hear. The doctor outlined plans for my treatment.

- First, I would have scans at Mission Hospital to see if there was cancer anywhere else in my body.
- I would be scheduled for out-patient surgery to have a port inserted for chemotherapy treatments.

- I would meet with an oncologist to discuss those treatments and attend a chemo class during which I would be advised of the drugs I would be taking.

This information was overwhelming with the doctor sharing so many details. Why did he think it necessary to tell me all this? What was he talking about? Who was he talking about? I did not need all these details! He could not be talking about me!

January 19, 2017: Alan and Drake came from Southport to see us. Their visit brought fresh air to a world smothered in angst.

January 21, 2017: We met our Knoxville family in Pigeon Forge where DJ treated us to a feast at the Apple Barn. The visit with them was another dose of the best kind of medicine – a supportive family. Their love covered me like a warm blanket on a dark, cold night; their laughter brought a glimmer of light to the darkness. They gave me so many reasons to fight this monster named breast cancer. A cancer diagnosis is not only a personal challenge. A loving family takes the pain and carries it with you.

January 22, 2017: It was nice to have Alan and Drake attend church with us. Each Sunday we have prayer time during the service when those present offer praises, express concerns and make prayer requests. Pastor George Davis asked David and me to come forward for prayer. He advised the congregation of what we were facing and asked anyone who wished to do so to come and stand with us. The out-pouring of love we experienced in that moment was awe-inspiring. There was not one person left sitting in the pews. Everyone in that congregation surrounded us at the altar. Pastor George's heartfelt prayer brought peace, comfort and strength. He prayed that there would be no evidence of cancer anywhere else in my body when the scans were performed.

On our drive to the mall that afternoon, Drake looked at me and asked, "Grandma, do you know what the best part of today is?"

"No, honey, what it is?" I asked.

His sweet response melted my heart, "You!" He smiled brightly.

January 24, 2017: In the 70 years of my life, I had been blessed to have only a tonsillectomy when I was in fourth grade, an appendectomy when I was a senior in high school, two pregnancies and a tubal ligation.

Going to the hospital for scans was daunting. I arrived on time, wearing my brave mask with my dear David walking by my side.

Upon our arrival, the first procedure took only half an hour. Dye was injected for the complete bone scan I would have about four hours later. While we waited for this dye to do its thing, I went to the radiation lab for upper and lower body CT scans.

As I drank the "cocktail" necessary prior to the scans (definitely not my Southern sweet tea), my phone buzzed. The text was a You Tube message of precious four-year-old Claire Ryann sweetly singing to her dad, "You Got a Friend in Me." The message came from Dave and Donna Dupree, dear friends in Arlington, Texas, to say they were thinking of and praying for me this very minute. Their timing could not have been more perfect. This act of kindness helped the drink to go down. I was grateful for that "God wink."

As I lay on the scan bed underneath the dome that hovered closely over me, my heart sang *The Sound of Music* and *Over the Rainbow* to keep my anxiety at bay. Those are two of my favorite songs.

During the bone scan, which was a long process, I silently sang hymns from my heart in alphabetical order: *Amazing Grace, Blessed Assurance, Come and Dine, Do Lord, Every Day With Jesus, Fill My Cup, Lord, Grace, Grace, God's Grace, Heaven Will Surely Be Worth It All, Isn't He Wonderful, Just As I Am, Kumbaya, Love Lifted Me, Must Jesus Bear the Cross Alone, Nothing But the Blood, Open My Eyes, Lord, People Need the Lord, There Is A Quiet Place, Rescue The Perishing, Sweet Hour of Prayer, Trust and Obey, Undeserving of His Love, Victory in Jesus*. Ending with *Wonderful Words of Life*, I was glad the scan was over as I don't know what I would have come up with for X, Y and Z.

The technician who did the scan urged, "Mrs. Bass, you must be still during the scans. If you move, we may have to repeat them." Between songs, I pleaded, "God, please help me not to move. Help me to be still." I should have quoted Psalm 46:10, *"Be Still and Know That I Am God."*

When the scan was complete, I asked the technician, "Did I do alright and stay still enough during the scans?"

He said, "Maam, you were like a statue."

Hospital staff looked for me and found me in the cardiology lab having an echo-cardiogram with a chest x-ray to follow. They said I needed to have another CT scan. My heart sank as I thought they had found a problem. But the technician had failed to do an upper scan that had been ordered. With a deep sigh, I started to breathe once more.

I told this technician I was going to silently sing again as she did the scan as that helped to calm my nerves. She sweetly responded, "Just belt 'em out."

But I told her I would do them silently. Laying very still, I sang, *Jesus, Jesus, There's Just Something About That Name*. The song brought comfort on that cold slab in that cold room.

That night David and I attended a service called "Healing Prayer," conducted at Grace Episcopal Church by Pastor David Warren, the one who met with us to pray before my appointment with Dr. Harkness. During this service, I wrote my concerns on a prayer card which was passed on to prayer warriors present. Each person placed their hands on my head and prayed for me. This time was so meaningful. Silent prayers from sincere hearts and those spoken aloud were powerful – further confirmation that many prayers would continue to go up on my behalf. God would hear every prayer. We continued to attend these Tuesday night services and gained encouragement and strength from all of them.

January 25, 2017: On Wednesday we met with Dr. Rachel Raab, Oncologist, to discuss chemotherapy. She came highly recommended; and those who commended her were right on target. She was thoughtful and encouraging. Her expertise in breast malignancies was evident; and her caring, compassionate attitude put me at ease. While we were in her office, her secretary came in with the results of my scans done the day before. She opened the folder and silently read the reports. With a smile bigger than life, she announced, "All the scans are clear. There is no sign of cancer anywhere else in your body."

I stood, gave two thumbs up, and declared aloud, "Thank You, Jesus!"

The doctor gave me a big hug. David held me in his arms; and we did not keep the tears of relief at bay. We let them fall freely from thankful hearts. She explained that on Tuesday, February 1, we were scheduled to attend a chemotherapy class for the two us, since no two cancer cases are exactly alike. We would meet with a nurse practitioner who would explain the pros, cons, benefits and side effects of two chemo drugs combined. Adriamycin and Cytoxan, known as the "Red Devil," fiercely attack cancer cells.

On hearing this information, my heart sank. Forty years ago, I had worked as the tumor registrar at Asheville VA Medical Center. Adriamycin and Cytoxan were two of the drugs they used in 1977. I wondered, "Have they not improved treatment since then?"

I asked why I could not go ahead and have surgery. I would prefer to have a complete mastectomy and get rid of the cancer. Having heard horror stories on the issue, I did not want to go through chemotherapy. Dr. Raab said I needed to have chemo to hopefully shrink the tumor before going into surgery.

January 26, 2017: Kathy Stepp, a dear friend who worked with me in *House of Lloyd*, answered my ad to become a demonstrator. But she became much more – one of my dearest friends, a sister from another mother. For a time, she worked with me at the Cove. She is now also an Avon representative and during our lunch on this day she loaded me with gifts relating to breast cancer awareness: A courage cup, sunglasses, two necklaces, an ornament, a watch and two bracelets. This precious friend is the kind that cannot do enough for those she loves and cares about, the kind anyone would be blessed to call "friend" or "adopted sister."

My follow-up appointment with Dr. Caldwell went well. Considering the stress I was under, my blood pressure was great. The kind staff assured me again of their prayers.

I met Margaret and Ron en route to a couple's retreat and delivered cancer awareness gifts from Kathy to her. As a twin herself, this friend knows the bond of twinship. She knew Margaret was hurting, too, and wanted her to know she cared.

January 27, 2017: I went to the Billy Graham Training Center, The Cove, in Asheville, where I had served as a dining room hostess, to say hi to friends. My supervisors Rita Harris and Deanna Sales took me to their office and prayed with me. Bill Solomon, a retired minister and coworker, prayed for me as well.

Following my retirement from the VA Medical Center, I worked at the Cove for a number of years and cherish memories I made there. I was privileged to meet popular guest speakers as well as those attending events. Co-workers became like family. William (Will) Graham, Billy Graham's grandson, and Gigi, his daughter, became dear to me, always making me feel special.

I will never forget a day in October 2001, just after I started working at the Cove. While a group of us sat at a table downstairs folding napkins, Dr. Billy Graham walked into the room and thanked us for our service. Meeting this outstanding man of God (America's pastor) is a memory I will cherish.

When I left the Cove, I stopped by to see Margaret Roberts, another dear friend. She had been a former neighbor years ago. When she moved, we lost contact. We reconnected on Facebook. Then she started working at the Cove with me. This once neighbor, now friend became another sister from another mother. "Sis" loaded my car with food: Chicken casserole, spaghetti, beef stew, broccoli salad, cornbread and pecan pie. It all looked so good. "Oh, God," I, prayed, "Please don't let me lose my appetite. I want to enjoy this food."

Jean Penland called to ask David and me to join her and Don for supper at Tommy's. We enjoyed a pleasant evening with another couple we are blessed to call friends.

January 28, 2017: Margaret and Ron came by from the retreat they had attended at the Methodist Assembly Grounds in Lake Junaluska, North Carolina. We enjoyed BLTs for lunch; then shopped at Hamrick's. That evening they treated David and me to a delicious meal at Cheddar's. Back at home, we enjoyed popcorn and the movie, "Mermaid."

Margaret brought encouraging sayings that Christy had printed out for me. I want to share a few of them. They brought more strength to me than she will ever know.

"You never know how strong you are until being strong is the only choice you have."

"You were given this life because you are strong enough to live it."

"They say what doesn't kill you makes you stronger. At this point, my dear, I should be able to bench-press a Buick."

January 29, 2017: At Emma Church, Margaret and I sang *I Know Who Holds Tomorrow* by Ira Stanphill:

Verse 1

I don't know about tomorrow;
I just live from day to day.
I don't borrow from its sunshine
for the skies may turn to gray.
I don't worry o're the future,
for I know what Jesus said.
And today I'll walk beside Him
for He knows what is ahead.

Chorus

Many things about tomorrow
I don't seem to understand.
But I know who holds tomorrow
and I know who holds my hand.

Verse 2

Every step is getting brighter
as the golden stairs I climb.
Every burden's getting lighter;
every cloud is silver lined.

There the sun is always shining.
There no tear will dim the eye
at the ending of the rainbow,
where the mountains touch the sky.[1]

The congregation brushed away tears as my twin and I sang from our hearts. I was carrying a load heavier than I had ever known; Margaret was trying to lessen my load by sharing it. Both of us knew that God would walk with us through the journey ahead, to the very last mile.

Though miles apart, closely tied with the bond of twinship, each of us knew we would not be alone. That song became my theme song and carried me through many difficult moments, hours, days and weeks.

January 30, 2017: My insurance agent and special friend, Cynthia Wilcox, asked if she could stop by and pray with David and me. Her visit was uplifting, another confirmation that I would not make this journey alone. Not only would God walk with me, He would send "His agents" to walk with me when I needed extra strength. Before she left, this precious lady stood in our living room and started to sing, *There's a Sweet, Sweet Spirit In This Place.* As I joined her in harmony, a peace that passes understanding engulfed me.

Time and again I was seeing how God works in mysterious ways His wonders to perform. Bringing peace, healing and hope to my troubled world, not only was He holding my tomorrow; He was holding me.

January 31, 2017: David took me to Mission Hospital for out-patient surgery to have a port inserted for chemo treatments. Using a local anesthesia, a small incision was made to insert the port under my skin on the left side of my

---

[1] I know who holds tomorrow; Author: Ira F. Stanphill, © 1950, renewed 1978, Singspiration Music; used by permission.

chest since the cancer was in my right breast. The port is the size of a quarter. A soft thin tube called a catheter connected the port to a large vein near my heart and a needle was passed through the skin into the port to push chemotherapy into the vein. Insertion of the port went well with no complications.

I was awake when I got to the operating room and knew when they moved me on to the table. When the OR nurse put an ice pack on my leg, I said, "Oh, that's what I've always wanted, something very cold on my leg!"

The surprised man responded, "Dr. Harkness, where did you find this woman? She's got spunk." My first experience with Dr. Harkness as my surgeon was a good one.

When we first moved to Asheville, we rented an apartment from Jean Penland's father. She became my first friend in Asheville. Later she and I worked together at the VA Medical Center. This first friend who had become a forever friend, came to sit with David during this procedure. I had no idea she was coming and was surprised to see her walk into my cubicle in the OR waiting area. I was in the recovery room with David beside me, wondering when they were going to insert the port... and it had already been done!

When I got home from the hospital, David's brother, Kenneth, arrived with enough food to feed an army. My sister-in-law, Marsha, and her two sisters, Diane and Donna, had prepared food to be enjoyed now with enough leftovers to be put in the freezer for future meals. The love and concern shown to us by family, friends, neighbors, church family and Cove co-workers were deeply appreciated. I was beginning to wonder where we would put all the food! The reality of my plight was becoming more real every day. Treatment and procedure plans presented to us were happening fast.

February 1, 2017: David and I went to the chemo class. Linda, the nationally certified nurse practitioner, involved in oncology for over 26 years, knew her "stuff." She spared no punches, painted no pretty picture and told us many things we could expect from my upcoming treatment: Side effects of nausea, vomiting, fatigue, hair loss, loss of appetite and taste were among the possibilities I might experience once the treatment was begun. She assured me that while I may not experience all of these, I needed to be aware of them.

When I told Linda about my song, *I Know Who Holds Tomorrow*, she agreed that it was a perfect choice and commended me for my positive attitude. She assured us that attitude was a big part of the battle ahead. My first treatment would be the "Red Devil." From my experience as a tumor registrar, I knew it was MEAN. She gave us a spiral bound notebook covering the information she had given us but suggested that we not read it immediately. We had enough to digest from today's class. We were given a tour of the chemo lab, which would make us familiar with the place and be helpful when I came for my first treatment.

February 5, 2017: At Emma Church, Pastor George Davis said a couple of people needed extra grace and asked David and me to serve communion that day. This kind gesture and opportunity to do something meaningful was an honor, a privilege and a blessing. God knew we needed it.

Brenda Maxwell, a precious sister in Christ, asked me to walk with her to her car so she could give me something. It was normally called a rag quilt but she had named this one a prayer quilt as she had prayed for me with every stitch. The fact that she had taken time not only to make this quilt but to pray for me meant more than she can ever know. Prior to my situation, her husband, Bob, had to have surgery; and complications required more surgery. This dear friend was strong and confident in her faith. I told her I didn't know how she did it and that if I ever had to experience something like that, I didn't know how I would get through it. She responded, "Martha, you could do it. I know you and I know you could." Little did she know what a prediction she had made that day.

David and I met the Bass family at Cracker Barrel in Hickory. They expressed concern and assured me of their prayers. Ellon, David's sister, and her husband Paul brought a gift card to Chick Fil A, a book, *What Cancer Cannot Do*, a breast cancer necklace and pen. Ken and Marsha gave me a praying angel to remind me that they, along with my niece, Tiffany, were praying for me.

From many places and people, love was being poured out daily. Despite all of it, the **return to reality** was not the happiest place I had ever been.

4

Facing the "Red Devil"

February 6, 2017: Monday morning I walked into the chemo lab wearing a button-down shirt (as I was instructed to do), carrying a bag with a book, a snack and the beautiful prayer quilt Brenda Maxwell had made for me. David was walking by my side.

As a tumor registrar at the VA Medical Center in Asheville, forty plus years ago, I watched many cancer victims come to the chemotherapy clinic every week. I had made the statement that if I were ever given a cancer diagnosis, I hoped I would never have to take chemo. I had heard the words Adriamycin and Cytoxan even back then. Hearing them now was stressful. Yet here I was ready to be put in a chair to do something I never thought I would have to do. Seated in the first chair on the front row, knowing poisonous chemicals were about to be shot into my body, I demanded panic to go!

Debra, my chemo nurse, had phoned me on Friday to let me know she would be taking care of me today and say I was in her thoughts and prayers during this treatment and the days ahead. She explained that she would first insert the needle into the port to draw blood for lab work before the treatment started. This was going to be a long day. She put a mask on my face and I took my first scary step on the chemo journey. I was about to face the "Red Devil" head on. But I surprised the monster; I smiled at my precious nurse and thanked her for being there for me.

Around the room, chemo chairs were filling. I was not taking this journey alone. Others joined me on the battlefield; all of us fighting to win this war. I am thankful that I put on my shield of faith God had provided for me; otherwise, the scene would have been too frightening to face.

What a pleasant surprise to see Debbie Walsher, my friend from the Cove, come into the chemo lab to see me and cheer me on. She had taken this journey a year ago, sat in this same lab with the same drugs being shot into her body; and she had won the battle! She gave me a book and pen to journal my experiences, along with plastic forks and spoons to use when it was difficult to eat due to "chemo mouth." She knew all too well what I was about to face; and her encouragement was invaluable.

After the day of treatment, a Neulasta Onpro body injector was placed on the side of my abdomen. This was a device I would wear for 27 hours. It would inject medicine to help prevent infection due to the low blood count I would get from the chemo drugs. I chose to wear this device rather than have to come back to the chemo lab the next day and get a shot in my stomach to inject the medicine. I was instructed to take the injector out precisely at the appointed time and take it immediately to a pharmacy where someone would dispose of it there.

Good news after the first treatment: There were no complications during the process and no side effects after it! I could do this! There was really no choice. I had to do this!

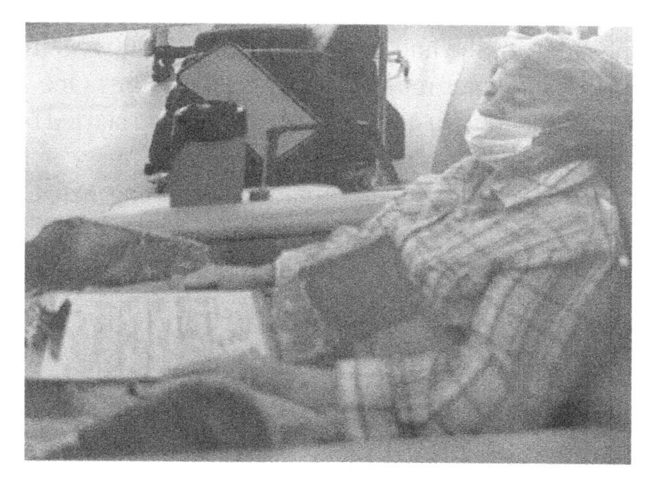

In the chemo chair

February 13, 2017: I went to the lab at Hope Cancer Center for follow-up blood work. As expected, some of the counts were low but not so low that we could not make a trip to our Southport haven. Erin Schmidt, the family nurse practitioner who had seen me, encouraged it as she believed it would lift my spirits. She was right. Seeing Alan and Drake, watching our little guy swim and taking it easy were doses of medicine for my body and my mind.

With precautions given by Erin, I was told to avoid hugs or even shaking hands with anyone. David and I had been given permission to attend the 70th wedding anniversary celebration for his Uncle Ben and Aunt Edna. He had sung at our wedding in December 1967. It meant so much to be with them for this milestone. We left Southport Sunday and stopped in Fayetteville for the event. Explaining my issue with chemo, I avoided hugs and handshakes as instructed. It was great to see so many of the Bass family, all of them assuring me of their love, support and prayers!

When we arrived in Asheville, my niece Christy had gotten there before us. She planned to accompany me to my second chemo treatment the following day. She had brought me a special gift. She had gotten the chest of drawers that had been in my precious mother's storage building. One of the drawers contained yarn and a shawl Mother had started but had not completed before she died. Tammy, Christy's friend, finished the shawl for me and made a matching hat. On one side of the shawl was a heart Mother had knitted. It was as though she reached down from heaven and gave me a hug.

The evening before my treatment, Christy and I enjoyed popcorn, a movie and chatting before going to bed. I was tired from the trip.

February 20, 2017: I took Christy to Cracker Barrel for breakfast before going to Hope Cancer Center. I saw Erin again on this visit and she measured the lump in my breast. She regrettably informed me that it appeared to be larger.

"No!" My heart silently screamed. "This is not what was supposed to happen. Chemotherapy was supposed to shrink this monster." Obviously, my assignment was to be patient. So off to the chemo lab I went, forcing hope to rise within me. I was told that someone would call me for an appointment for another ultrasound.

Just as David had done two weeks before, my dear niece sat with me during my treatment expressing words of love, encouragement and support. David came later that day so Christy could get back home to Charlotte and avoid heavy afternoon traffic. I thanked her for coming. Her being there meant so much to me.

February 21, 2017: Getting together with dear friends, Jean and Margaret, co-workers from the VA, was a treat. Being with them was refreshing. During this journey, I was learning that little things mean a lot. I felt so happy to still have my hair.

February 22, 2017: The next morning I awoke with hair all over my pillow. "What is this? This can't be happening!"

As I lathered my hair in the shower, it came out by the handfuls, falling around my feet in the tub. This was one of the most difficult moments of the journey so far. I had heard of patients losing their hair and felt bad for them. But there was no way I could have imagined their pain, which was real to me now. As tears streamed down my face, I prayed for strength. "God, I can't do this! You've got to help me!" Helpless, defeated and weak, reality hit me in the face. And I hated the "Red Devil."

Struggling to breathe, I recalled what a "cancer sister" had shared with me. During a low moment on her journey, she had said those same words, "God, I can't do this!" She said it seemed that God whispered to her, "No, you can't; but I can. Can you trust me?" From that moment, rather than think of her "Cancer," she decided to put her trust in God. Repeatedly she said to Him, "Yes, I can trust you, God. I can, Sir!"

David cleaned up the hair mess. He said, "Go on, honey, I am going to clean this up. You don't need to do that." I walked away, my body numb from the pain of the scene.

I called my hairdresser, Amanda, explained my situation and asked if I could come in for a short pixie cut. Tears streamed down the dear woman's face as she cut my hair while it continued to fall out. She did a great job with what little hair I had left. She refused payment. And on my way out, she assured me of her prayers.

A client who had just entered the shop came up to us and said she was pleased to hear someone not ashamed to mention prayer in public. I told her chemo had robbed me of my hair and Amanda had been my earth angel. The client, whose employee name badge read Ginger, said she would also be praying for me.

As I started to walk out, she called out to me, "Martha, wait a minute. Something just told me to give you this." She reached into her purse and handed me a $2 bill.

Tears streamed down my face as I responded, "Ginger, my dad used to do this often. He would put a $2 bill in a birthday or Christmas card. He left $2 bills in restaurants for tips. Many people today keep a $2 that special man gave them. I haven't gotten a $2 bill for a while now. Dad is waiting for us in heaven."

Ginger answered, "Well, then, it must have been your dad who told me to give you the $2 bill and he wants you to know everything is going to be alright."

Pixie Haircut (Compliments of Amanda)

As David and I walked to our car, we realized God had just winked at me again. My pixie haircut was short lived. I had been blessed with a head full of thick hair; but it continued to fall out. The next day I saw David walking into the house from the garage with the shop vac in his hand. He said, "Honey, you need to be vacuumed." And he proceeded to vacuum hair from my shoulders, back, arms and chest. This procedure was repeated more than once. Not every husband takes time to vacuum floors; let alone vacuum his wife.

I said, "Honey, you have more important things to do than vacuum your wife. I am going to get my head shaved."

February 23, 2017: This morning was hard as I got the news that LaNita Clark, my friend from Scaly Mountain, North Carolina had lost her battle with breast cancer. Knowing she had left this world for a better place helped to ease my pain. Catherine Coats, a co-worker from the Cove, dropped by. Knowing I enjoy them, she brought me Garrison Keillor audio cassette tapes to listen to. Seeing her was an uplift.

February 24, 2017: I phoned Amanda for an appointment to get my head shaved. This was not a happy day at all. I don't think anyone can prepare themselves for this harsh trip: The tiredness, acid reflux, heartburn, going bald. More and more, I felt resentment for the "Red Devil" that was wreaking havoc with my life. I was giving every ounce of energy I had to fight this battle; but today it felt like the monster was winning.

February 25, 2017: We rode to Knoxville, Tennessee where we were privileged to see our eleven-year-old grandson Luke receive honors in his Boy Scout Troop. We were so proud of him and enjoyed this time with our K-town family. Pam, Jamie's mom, and her friend, Robert, joined us. She brought me gifts of special Doterra oils I planned to try as soon as I got home. Katrinia, my sister-in-law, had knitted caps for me to wear on my slick-as-a-ribbon bald head. I was totally matching, green cap, green shirt and green slacks.

I received a gift package from Rhonda Daugherty: A "red-head" wig, Kleenex, a little doll to hug, a rope to tie a knot in. Rhonda was the daughter-in-law of my twin's former boss. When Margaret asked the Daughertys to pray for me, they shared my plight with Rhonda. She had taken the rough and rocky "C" journey and jumped many hurdles. This dear lady, whom I had never met, reached out to me with compassion and love that warmed my heart. I could not hold back tears, touched by the kindness of this stranger.

February 26, 2017: For an early birthday celebration on Sunday night, Roland, David's brother, Katrinia, his wife, and Sharon, his daughter, brought supper that looked appetizing: Fish, shrimp, fries from home-grown potatoes and coleslaw from home-grown cabbage.

Unfortunately, one of the effects of chemotherapy had kicked in. My taste was gone. "Chemo mouth," metal mouth, as it is also called, makes food taste so bad that cancer patients have to force themselves to eat at a time when they need nourishment most to help with recovery. What I am sure was delicious to those around me tasted like metal to me. The meal brought on horrendous acid reflux. Despite my hidden misery, I was thankful that everyone else enjoyed the meal. And we had a delightful visit.

Katrinia brought more hats and a brunette wig her mom had worn on her chemo journey. We paraded wigs and laughed. Proverbs 17:22 says laughter works like a medicine. And that's what this precious lady gave me that night. She is like a second sister. Her love and friendship have lifted me from the pits more times than she can ever know.

February 27, 2017: I went to the American Cancer Society where I was invited to select a free wig. I chose a cute short blond style. Despite the challenge I was fighting with acid reflux, the adventure brightened my day.

This journey was hard; so I determined to make the best of it. I could be a flaming red-head, a feisty brunette or even a platinum blond... And if I chose to go bald (as some do) as Andrea Hutton, the kind author so aptly recorded in her book, *Bald is better with earrings.*

February 28, 2017: I enjoyed the Beth Moore Bible Study at Emma Church. David and I attended another healing service at Grace Episcopal Church. These services were so meaningful for me and helped to get me through some rough spots; they kept me from falling.

March 1, 2017: At the suggestion of Janet McGregor, nurse navigator, I scheduled an appointment with Alice Myer at Hope Cancer Center. This was exactly what I needed. I was able to answer this counselor's questions honestly and openly. I poured my heart out to her as she listened with compassion. Her advice and encouragement brought me hope! Pictures on her wall helped me relax. I love scenic pictures that tell stories: A road leading to a farmhouse, another road through a covered bridge, a two-story house with a snow-covered lawn and a little white church with a steeple. I can get lost in landscapes.

March 2, 2017: David and I met Roland and Katrinia at Nara's, a Japanese restaurant, in Marion, North Carolina, one of my favorites. But due to horrific acid reflux, I ate very little.

As has become a tradition when we take this jaunt from Asheville, we shopped in Roses. Katrina gave me ideas for organizing my cancer gifts. Blessed, I was collecting many.

March 3, 2017: I had another ultrasound at Hope Cancer Center to determine the size of the cancer following chemo treatments. This was not the way I had planned to spend my 71st birthday. The radiologist gave a brief explanation that the tumor seemed to be bigger but said this could be the result of chemo as substance can show near the tumor making it appear to be larger. The doctor would meet with me at my next appointment on March 6 to go over the results. Hopefully, this was good news. David and I left feeling more confused than we were before the ultrasound. Having seen so many ill effects as a tumor registrar, now experiencing them myself, my preference was to stop chemo and proceed with surgery.

March 4, 2017: David and I went to Easley, South Carolina to share a birthday meal with extended family. Our first stop was the cemetery on Main Street. Wearing my shawl that had been made from her yarn with the heart, I thanked Mother for it. I thanked Dad for the $2 bill Ginger had given me and the message that I was going to be okay. As tears fell to the ground, I poured my heart out to my precious parents in heaven. I told them the cancer journey was hard, and I was scared. The scene in the cemetery is one that still lingers in my mind. David said as he watched and silently prayed, his heart was breaking for me and he would never forget it.

Margaret and Ron joined us at the grave site. She confessed to me later that she had a meltdown in the car when they got there. She told Ron she couldn't do this. She would see me for the first time with no hair and her heart was breaking. Ron prayed with her, told her she needed to do this and that with God's help, she could. She joined me at the grave, her soulmate following close behind her. Letting the tears flow freely, we both talked to Mother and Dad. She had allowed me private space; but she needed to talk to them, too.

They live on in my heart; I needed to talk to them

My wombmate told me she would have her head shaved; but I said absolutely not. She did not need to do that to prove she was with me “all the way.” She had her hair cut short and got matching wigs for us. She held the wig up; and as I slowly removed my cap, with tears gleaming in her eyes, she handed it to me. These were gray (like my natural hair had been). I added this gray one to my “wig wardrobe.”

Margaret and I put on our matching wigs and went to Fatz where Christy, cousins Kaye, Tia, Jimmy, Patsy and Aunt Irene were waiting to celebrate our birthday in a private room. They had brought a birthday cake and sweet birthday gifts (all of them dealing with breast cancer). Everyone made the evening special.

Margaret drove me back home to Asheville; and Ron rode with David. She and I enjoyed this twin time and the privilege to pour our hearts out to each other.

The twins in matching wigs

March 5, 2017: Ron and Margaret attended church with us at Emma. The three of us sang *Joy Comes in the Morning,* by Bill Gaither – appropriate words for this leg of the journey.

After Dad died, Mother visited often, sometimes for extended stays. We prepared a beautiful bedroom for her. She decorated it with an over-the-bed canopy and matching drapes. She had her own recliner and television. We called it "Nanny's Suite." It became my "comfort zone." I would sit in her recliner and somehow feel her near.

That Sunday afternoon Margaret and I sat in the Nanny Suite and watched a couple of Hallmark movies. Exhausted from the busy weekend, I fell asleep under the beautiful warm pink blanket (with the breast cancer symbol) she had brought me as a gift from Diane Fosdick, her pastor's wife.

March 6, 2017: I had looked forward to having Margaret meet my sweet Dr. Raab. What a disappointment to learn that she was not in that day and I would see another doctor. I had been promised that the results of the ultrasound would be discussed in detail; but this doctor provided little information. I told her what I wanted was for Dr. Harkness to go ahead and do the surgery. She said she would put that request in my chart and basically told me to go on for my next treatment. We left knowing nothing more than when we arrived.

My twin was fit to be tied. Disgusted and disappointed (just as I was), she went with me to the chemo lab. We met some kind new patients that day, exchanging words of courage and hope throughout the treatment.

Ron and Margaret shared a meal with us at Cracker Barrel in Hendersonville as they made their way home to Concord. As had become our custom, David and I headed back to Southport where we would spend several days following my treatment. These times in Southport had been good for me.

Spending time with Alan (who was staying in our home during this time) was like medicine. I could hardly believe my eyes when we walked in. The house was spotless. Our beach haven was so welcoming. He had done an amazing job getting it ready for us.

March 7, 2017: Holly, Drake's mother, was attending a conference in Raleigh so Drake got to spend the week with us. He fell asleep while I read him two bedtime stories. He is such a sweet child, respectful, thoughtful, kind, and another dose of medicine for me.

March 8, 2017: We picked Drake up early from pre-school, drove to Independence Mall in Wilmington and had lunch at the food court. Alan had a work conference call at 6 pm so Grandma and Grandpa enjoyed taking Drake to his swim lesson. He swims like a fish.

March 9, 2017: When Alan picked Drake up from school, we had supper. This trip to Southport was beginning to be different. The "Red Devil" had followed me there, gripping my body, beating me down. To say that chemo makes you feel fatigued is the understatement of the century. Extreme fatigue was overtaking me. My days were now spent asleep on the couch. Sometimes when I woke up, I didn't even know where I was.

March 10, 2017: Thankfully, I mustered enough strength to help Drake mix the batter for my birthday Paw Patrol cake and cupcakes. I also managed to fix hotdogs, chili and slaw (what I had wanted for my Southport birthday party). I ate a few chips and part of a hotdog but was not able to taste this birthday meal.

March 11, 2017: David and Denise Rowland, friends (aka our beach buddies) we had met from Margaret and Ron's church at Enochville, dropped by to see us. They own a place at Holden Beach and wanted to stop by while they were in the area. Their love, support and prayers mean so much. After they left, we rode to Wilmington. David and I sat in the truck while Alan and Drake went in the children's museum. The subs they picked up looked so good. I managed to get down part of one. Oh, if only I could have tasted it, life would have been so much better.

March 12, 2017: Holly came by to pick up Drake and brought me a beautiful birthday card. I also had one to give to her since she has a March birthday, too. In any situation where there is divorce, there is pain not only for the couple going their separate ways but also for both families involved. There were some unpleasant memories. But my relationship with my ex-daughter-in-law improved after my diagnosis. She was kind, considerate and thoughtful. I came to realize this was part of my healing; and for that I was grateful.

March 13, 2017: In addition to the extreme fatigue I experienced during this time, nausea and vomiting hit with a vengeance. Meds prescribed for that did nothing to help. In the wee hours of the morning, unable to make it to the bathroom, I had a horrendous accident and everything had to be changed. It was during those times, I was so thankful for a loving companion, who, just as he promised, was with me through every defying horrific moment.

March 14, 2017: That morning when I looked in the mirror, a stranger stared me in the face. I had no idea who this pitiful, ugly, bald-headed, thin little old lady was with sunken cheeks, ashen skin and trembling hands. I did not know her, nor did I want to. All I knew was that her name was Cancer. And I did not like her.

"The Cancer Poster Child"

I could never have made this scary journey without my dear family. The love and kindness shown to me by my soulmate and three sons (on days when I looked and felt my worse) gave me courage to keep fighting. I was the one posing as the "cancer poster child," but the love pierced with pain in

Alan's heart was mirrored on his face and could not be hidden. I saw it even through dark glasses.

I phoned Janet at Hope Cancer Center to tell her what was happening, pleading with her to help me get the chemo treatments stopped. She assured me that she would pass this information on to Dr. Raab.

March 17, 2017: We stopped in Concord for the night on our way home to Asheville. Ron had made his delicious salmon patties, with green peas and stewed potatoes, knowing this was one of my favorite menus. I was grateful for his kindness but could taste nothing.

March 18, 2017: After what I am sure was a delicious breakfast at Margaret and Ron's (though I could taste nothing), we headed to Asheville. David decided to drive through Chimney Rock as he knew it was one of my favorite places. It was a beautiful day and the lovely scenery lightened my darkness between naps.

March 19, 2017: After attending church at Emma, we went to Hardees where I attempted to eat a mushroom swiss burger (another favorite). But again that effort was futile. I slept most of the afternoon. Through a restless night, I prayed, begging God to let the appointment at Hope Cancer Center the next day be a good one.

March 20, 2017: My prayers were answered when Dr. Raab informed me that due to the horrible side effects I was experiencing from chemo, I was being delivered from the "Red Devil." There would be no more chemo. I had planned to tell her that I had already made that decision myself and would not take another treatment. What I really wanted to do was a happy dance; but I had no strength to do it.

To my further delight, a knock came on her door and Dr. Harkness walked in. She had phoned him and he was there to discuss my surgery. This is what I had wanted from the onset – a mastectomy to remove the dreadful cancer!

The medical staff had insisted on Plan A: To shrink the tumor with chemo prior to surgery. But that did not happen. Now they were willing to go with what had become Plan B: The mastectomy I had pled for from the beginning.

I received the final report of the ultrasound that was done on March 3. It read:

> There is a 6.1 x 5.5 x 4.4 oval mass with an angular margin in the right breast at 9:00 o'clock, 3 cm from the nipple. This mass previously measured 4.4 x 3.4 x 2.7 cm. This mass has a mixed solid/cystic appearance. Increase in size of this mass is due to increased size of the cystic components: The solid components and the associated vascularity have decreased from the prior ultrasound on January 3, 2017. The impression from this proven malignancy oval mass in the right breast has increased in size. This is due to increase in size of the cystic components."

The truth – the hard cold fact – was that the chemo treatment had not produced the results the medical team had hoped it would. The lump in my breast had not shrunk. It was not smaller. It was bigger.

I was thankful to know this dreadful cancer was going to finally be removed from my breast. Grateful and relieved that at least part of the journey was behind me, I left Hope Cancer Center with renewed hope that day.

But I could not stop the tears from coming. I let them fall freely. Overwhelmed, emotionally drained, sick, exhausted and weary from travelling, I realized that a "Cancer journey" is a devastating life-changing experience, not only for patients but also for those who love and care about them.

I was thankful to be alive. In **Facing the "Red Devil,"** I had been to hell and back.

5

Sensible Surgery

March 21, 2017: I was relieved to be scheduled for surgery. Today I prayed for my son Wayne, who was having an interview for a teaching position in Bloomington, Illinois. There was so much to look forward to with friends and family. With renewed hope, I looked ahead to an exciting future.

March 22, 2017: Kathy and I met for lunch and exchanged birthday gifts. I met with Alice again to discuss my upcoming surgery and admitted to her that the idea of losing one of my breasts did not make me happy but knowing the cancer would be gone did. I told her I knew that thousands of people had lost limbs and thousands of women had lost breasts; but the difference in this situation was that they had not lost mine. In the meantime, I was also praying that there would be no involvement in the lymph nodes.

March 23, 2017: We enjoyed another visit with Roland and Katrinia and our routine at Nara's. Even though chemo treatments were over, the chemo-mouth stayed around. Sadly, I could still taste nothing. At Roses Katrina helped me choose dresses that button in front as they would be more comfortable to wear after surgery.

March 24, 2017: The staff at Hope Cancer Center and Mission Hospital were thorough in their pre-op instructions. I had blood work for complete counts, a chest x-ray and an EKG – an all-day affair.

March 25, 2017: The drive to pick Wayne up at the airport in Greenville, South Carolina was a pleasant one. When we got back to Asheville, some of my heroes had arrived: DJ, John and Luke. Grace had band competition; Jamie stayed behind with her. Alan and Drake planned to come after I got home from the hospital. Just as I knew they would, my family was there to support me to the battle's end.

March 26, 2017: Having my family with me in church was a blessing too deep for words. For lunch Wayne made gravy biscuits with sausage, eggs and grits. I longed to taste that delicious meal and was so disappointed that I couldn't. That afternoon DJ, John and Luke returned to Knoxville with plans for DJ to return Monday when he got off work.

March 27, 2017: Wayne took me to my hypertension appointment with Dr. Caldwell and was thankful to meet the physician I had spoken so highly of over the years. This dear man had gotten my high blood pressure readings on track. Today's reading was a bit high but to be expected with what lay ahead. As was his custom, this Christian doctor prayed with me before I left. His kind words spoken to God on my behalf still linger in my heart.

March 28, 2017: The day for the long-awaited **sensible surgery** had finally arrived. When I got up that morning, David, DJ and Wayne were there to encourage and lift me up. Ron and Margaret arrived mid-morning, bringing food to put in the freezer for when I got home from the hospital.

We arrived at Mission hospital at 1:00 p.m. Since Pastor George and his wife Billie were away on a pre-planned vacation, David Warren was in the waiting room when we arrived. Jean Penland and Margaret Roberts were already there. Roland, Katrinia, Ellon, Paul and Christy joined those present for the event. In addition, Kenneth and Wayne Rouse, friends of Ron and Margaret who were in Asheville, asked if they could drop by. The love and support I felt that day were overwhelming. While I would undergo surgery, 15 members of "Team Martha" would be on the sidelines cheering the medical team and me on.

Only a couple of people could go with me to the surgical area. Others could come two at a time to speak with me before I went to the operating room. I asked that my precious David and Margaret go with me first.

At 2:00 p.m. I was scheduled to be taken to radiology for a sentinel node biopsy – a surgical procedure done to remove samples of lymph nodes to be tested for breast cancer cell metastases. The procedure was uncomfortable, thankfully performed by a kind staff. I told them God was going with me through every phase of this journey and they agreed. They said they saw Him in my smile.

On my way back to the surgical waiting area, I passed Wayne and Margaret sitting on a bench, talking. They smiled and waved. Their smiles brightened when I smiled back.

It was peace that passes understanding that engulfed me as I waited to be taken to the operating room. Friends and family waited patiently downstairs to come and spend a brief moment with me. Two by two they came, amazed at my humor, laughter and the calmness I projected even before any pre-op meds had been administered.

There was so much going on around me – nurses doing their thing and anesthetists assuring me that I would be sound asleep. My dear surgeon came to remind me again that he would be performing a total mastectomy. In addition, he would remove lymph nodes that would be biopsied following the surgery. Ellon and Ron were with me when Dr. Harkness came to talk with me.

As I was wheeled away to the operating room just after 4:00 p.m., the "core gang" (David, DJ, Wayne, Margaret, Ron, Christy, Roland and Katrinia) stood on the sidelines, their smiles bigger than life, bidding me go. At that moment, I knew the reality of 1 John 4:18: *Perfect love casts out fear.*

With God's arms wrapped around me, surrounded by love of my family, there was no reason to be afraid. Furthermore, what was about to take place was the most sensible thing that had happened on this journey. The unwanted cancer in my body was about to be removed!

In the operating room, I told the staff I was in God's hands and that He would use them as His instruments to do what they needed to do to take care of me. As I closed my eyes, I sensed HIS presence; He was holding me. The next thing I knew, I looked up and saw a nurse sitting at a desk beside me. In a quiet, husky voice, I asked, "Where am I?"

In a sweet voice, she answered, "Mrs. Bass, you are in the recovery room. Your surgery is over. You did great."

Soon after I was awake, my family started coming to the recovery room to see me. First came David, DJ and Wayne.

As Margaret and Ron were walking in, her phone beeped. Dr. Tim Hill, General Overseer of the Church of God, was calling to see how I was doing. That morning she had called his office to tell his assistant I was having surgery and ask her to have him pray for me. Perfect timing. He will never know how much his call meant to my family and me.

When Roland and Katrina came, she promised to make me her tasteful cream of cauliflower soup, which I love. Thinking about that made my heart smile.

I was in recovery longer than usual because they had to wait for a regular room to come available for me. Family and friends started to leave the hospital when they realized I was doing well. Some had quite a distance to travel. David stayed the night with me. Margaret and Ron went to our house with Wayne. DJ headed home to Knoxville.

Supporters at the hospital

Being in the hospital is no fun with nurses constantly doing what they need to do: Taking vitals, delivering pills… They were attentive, considerate, the best! David was nearby to hear my every whim and do whatever I needed him to do.

March 29, 2017: I didn't eat much for breakfast. Hospital food is not my favorite cuisine; "no-taste" was no issue. David Warren stopped by just after my David went home to get a nap. Margaret, Ron and Wayne arrived shortly afterward. Encouraging me to eat, Wayne helped to feed me some collard greens, sweet potatoes and barbeque. Knowing I needed to eat, I allowed him to do that and forced myself to do it for him.

It was a bit low before surgery and my blood count had gone lower since surgery. Before I could be discharged, I was given two units of blood (my first time ever to receive a blood transfusion).

Margaret could not believe I was being discharged one day after a mastectomy. When the nurse came in to say I was doing well and would be going home soon, she exclaimed, "What? Today? She just had major surgery!"

The nurse explained that for insurance reasons, patients were discharged as soon as possible and that some women who had undergone mastectomies in the morning had been discharged that afternoon. Margaret accepted the explanation, responding to the nurse with kindness; but the look on her face told me she was appalled. I could clearly read her eyes and heard her silently screaming, "You have got to be kidding!"

Knowing I would be going home soon, my twin and Ron headed home to Concord. I knew it was hard for her to leave but also knew she would be coming back soon.

At 6:30 p.m. I was released from the hospital. Wayne and David got me home to Panorama Drive. Apparently, being in my own bed was good for me. I slept from 11:00 p.m. til 11:00 a.m. the next day, the best 12 hours' sleep I had enjoyed for a long time.

6

The Road to Recovery

March 30, 2017: It was good to be home and especially to have Wayne, Alan and Drake with us. Drake couldn't understand why Grandma was sick. He seemed so sad; but we explained to him that I had just come home from the hospital and had to get a lot of rest. In January he had to have surgery for a hernia. Alan explained to him that Grandma had to have something really bad taken out of her boob and reminded him of how careful he had to be after he had his surgery.

Drake gave me a gentle hug and said, "Grandma, I am so sorry you had to have that hernia taken out of your boob." The little guy sure enjoyed being with his Uncle Wayne.

David, who had become my rock, and my twin sons took good care of me during my post-operative days. David and Wayne helped to empty drainage tubes and attended to any other medical issues that had to be done. Alan prepared meals and made sure I got my needed rest.

In trying to prepare myself for what would follow after surgery, I had read all I could about it. I knew about drainage tubes; but even having read and heard about them from other cancer patients I had no idea how annoying they would be – a pain to deal with!

Two drains, long tubes, were inserted into my breast area and armpit to collect fluid that can accumulate in the space where the tumor was. The tubes had plastic bulbs on the ends to create suction, which helped the fluid to exit my body. The fluid was red at first (blood). Then it changed colors. For the sake of the reader, I will omit further gory details here. Not only did I have to deal with the monstrosity of the tubes themselves, I had to keep a record of the amount of fluid. Even though I have been labeled as an excellent organizer, secretary and fact keeper, at this point in my life, I was not in the mood for detailed reports.

I could never have made it through "the drain chapter" without the help of my brave David and my son Wayne. During one of the darkest chapters of my journey, their unconditional love and support shone like a dim light at the end of a long tunnel.

Another thing I had not prepared myself for was grief that would be part of the healing process after losing a breast. In my research, I read where Becky Zuckweiler described five stages of anticipatory grief:

1. **Denial**
   Nature's way of cushioning us from reality
2. **Protest**
   Anger, sadness, confusion
3. **Disorientation**
   Physical symptoms of stress (normal)
4. **Detachment**
   Isolation and withdrawal
5. **Resolution**
   A renewed state of reorganization and acceptance

March 31, 2017: This was a bad day. The saying I've heard since I can remember is that the third day after surgery is the worst. You could prove it by me! This third day was my worst so far. I felt sluggish and had no energy. This was partly due to the fact that the anesthesia had completely worn off and pain was much more noticeable. In the midst of the physical pain, perhaps my heaviest load that day was depression. In appreciation for all the love and care being shown to me, I fought to keep my tears at bay. But there were moments when I thought the dam would break. And if it had, I don't know that I could have stopped it.

During this journey, Alan had ordered "Team Martha" shirts. He had taken orders from friends and family who wished to purchase a t-shirt and join the team to help me fight this battle. On the day after I returned home from the hospital, I walked into the living room where David, Wayne, Alan and Drake stood wearing their shirts. Surprised, overwhelmed and at a loss for words, immediately I started to receive text messages expressing love and support, photos of individuals posing in their shirts. Many people had supported me with love and kindness on this journey. But I had no idea that in the wings and on the front line more than 30 people had officially joined "Team Martha" (had the shirt to prove it) and were engaged in warfare, fighting this battle with me to the end.

April 1, 2017: Saturday came all too soon. My boys told me they had to go. It was not a sick April Fool joke. They really had to leave. Alan took Wayne to the airport to fly to San Diego and he and Drake would continue the drive back to Southport. They had been my shining stars; and I would never forget what they did for me. I missed them so much. But my David did not have to leave; he continued to be my rock.

Team Martha

April 2, 2017: I did not feel like going to church; but this afternoon I rode with David to Arby's just to get out of the house. I was hungry for a roast beef sandwich; but to my disappointment, I still could not taste it. I know God is bringing healing to me day by day. But when will this end? "Please, God," I begged, "Let me taste food again. It looks so good; but eating is becoming a chore."

My precious dad was on my mind a lot today. If he were still on earth, he would have celebrated his 93rd birthday. I miss him.

April 3, 2017: Margaret Roberts brought David a delicious-looking chocolate cake. I said it was delicious looking because there was no way I could taste it. I would simply have to trust its looks. While she was here, we had a horrific thunderstorm. It represented my status at the moment. I was in a storm, in a dark place looking up to see the bottom.

I could not taste cake (or anything else for that matter). This was one of those moments when I forced myself out of the pit and said, "You can't stay here, you've got to move on."

God sends sunshine after rain. Later that day Brenda, from Dr. Harkness' office, called with great news. No cancer was found in the lymph nodes. Margins were clear. That evening David's brother, Ken, brought more food. Even though I could not taste it, I knew that one day I would taste again. I had asked God to let that happen; and He is faithful.

April 4, 2017: Derek and Martha Ledford, friends from Emma Church, who had become like family to us, brought lunch. Martha's home-made chicken salad is a favorite of mine. We had a delightful visit. As they were leaving, Ron and Margaret arrived for a surprise over-night visit. They had spent the day at Biltmore enjoying their annual pass. But I had no idea they were coming. She and I enjoyed watching "Driving Miss Daisy" while Ron and David watched another movie downstairs.

April 5, 2017: Margaret and Ron had breakfast with us. She made omelets, biscuits and fries that looked delicious; but my longing to taste still taunted me. They headed home as we left for my appointment with Dr. Harkness. Thankfully, one of the drainage tubes was removed and I saw in print the news that had been told to me earlier: No cancer in lymph nodes, margins clear. In His time and in His way, God was answering prayer! One day I would taste again.

April 6, 2017: I met with Dr. Condra, a radiologist, to discuss the possibility of radiation once the surgery site had completely healed. She wanted me to meet with Dr. Raab to discuss further chemo, explaining that these treatments were insurance and defensive measures to prevent the invasive cancer I had from recurring. This would be a big decision. Was I supposed to take the treatments or was I supposed to trust God to do total healing? Remembering my ghastly experience with chemo, hearing that word was the last thing I needed that day. I prayed that God would give me peace. The confusion screaming in my head was deafening.

The positive note of the day was that the second drainage tube was removed – a blessing for which I was grateful – a light flickering in a dark moment. And the day got better. Cathy Jackaway, a friend from church, came and cleaned my house. That evening Katrina brought the cream of cauliflower soup she had promised me when I was in the hospital. In the midst of this painful journey with so many unexpected curves, I was being treated like royalty.

April 7, 2017: Deanna Sales from the Cove brought soups, casseroles, salads and breads. The continued outpouring of love was overwhelming. We found ourselves asking what would be delivered next.

April 8, 2017: Pastor Warren brought McKenna, his precious 16-year-old granddaughter to see me. She was visiting from Statesville. She was a little girl when her granddad pastored our church and when her family came to visit, I was her Sunday School teacher. She brought me a bouquet of flowers. The vase would become even more special in the future as you will learn.

April 9, 2017: It was good to be in church at Emma. During prayer time, I expressed my gratitude for being cancer free. Having been given permission from Dr. Harkness, after church we headed to Southport. We took the route through Mocksville so we could stop at K&W (a favorite dining spot). I had looked forward to the country-style steak. Cruel chemo-mouth was still doing its thing; but the steak had a hint of taste, a reason to hope that the answer to that prayer was on its way. Thanks to Alan, our Southport haven was again clean as a pen. Being there for a couple of weeks would be a refuge from the storm raging within me. Questions were rearing their ugly heads demanding answers that I did not have.

April 11, 2017: Drake came over for a visit and seeing our grandson was a treat. Margaret and Ron had come to their place down the street and she wanted to make dinner for us. Being the kind of person that has walked through life running, I thought now that my surgery was over, I could run again. WRONG. Margaret was preparing "Huntersville hamburgers" for supper (a traditional family treat). I had volunteered to make slaw. When I went to our kitchen island to do that, I was so weak I was trembling. It was hard to breathe. I don't remember ever being that tired (even with chemo). It was obvious that I had over done my efforts at post-op recovery. When we got to Margaret's, she took one look at me and said, "You eat, get home and go straight to bed!" And that's exactly what I did. I had learned my lesson. Now I knew that recovery comes slowly. That would mean taking it easy, being nice to myself; but for me, that would **not** be easy.

April 13, 2017: David and I went to the Montessori School to watch Drake ride in a Trike-a-Thon to raise money for St. Jude Hospital. Our little man did a great job on his little trike. I came home and rested.

April 14, 2017: On Good Friday, David and I enjoyed an early supper at Ron and Margaret's. Then she and I toured an inspiring Easter presentation, "A Trip to the Cross," at Beach Road Baptist Church nearby.

April 15, 2017: We rode over to Little River, South Carolina with Ron and Margaret and ate at Matthews Pancake House. After browsing in Nick Nack's in Calabash where we purchased their famous fudge, we came back home. I took a 2½ hour nap. Having promised myself I would not overdo it again; I intended to keep that promise.

April 16, 2017: We attended service at Trinity UMC in Southport and afterwards enjoyed lunch on our screened in porch. It was a relaxing Easter Sunday afternoon, a great day to enjoy a movie with my twin and leftovers for supper.

April 17, 2017: I made breakfast for Ron and Margaret as they were heading home to Concord. Monday night Alan treated David and me to a meal at Jones Seafood Restaurant.

April 18, 2017: David and I made a Shallotte run with breakfast at Waffle House, a stop in Lowe's, Bath and Body Works and Great Clips. David got a haircut. It would be a while before I would need one.

We were sad to learn from Pastor George that Vernon Lloyd, another member of Emma Church, had died. Ken Ledford had died on the day of my surgery. His memorial service would be held on Saturday and Vernon's on Monday.

The rest of our time in Southport was restful. I visited Fort Caswell where I used to work in food service. We took a drive down to the end of Oak Island. I did some light cleaning and started to prepare for our return trip to Asheville.

April 25, 2017: I went for my follow-up appointment with Dr. Raab. She explained that the chemotherapy Taxol is the standard treatment following a mastectomy. It is different from the "Red Devil;" side effects are not nearly as rough. She was pleased with how my incision looked and said I was healing well. She suggested that I wait two more weeks before making a decision regarding treatment.

April 27, 2017: We had a nice breakfast at Bojangles. Later in the day, I had an unpleasant experience. Apparently, according to personality studies I've seen and read, I am a slow boiler. I rarely lose my temper. But when something trips my trigger, I lose it. I blow up. When that happens, I become the epitome of a drama queen. That happened today.

Margaret shared a story with me a few years ago that helped me to deal with the overwhelming kindness being shown to me. There were times when I felt like saying, "Oh, no, you don't need to do that."

Once someone had given Margaret something and she told them they didn't need to do that. They responded, "You mean you are going to cheat me out of the blessing God wants to give me for helping you? What you really need to say is, Thank you, I appreciate that so much." What my twin shared with me helped me to realize that's what I needed to do.

As an act of kindness, someone had offered to come help me with anything I needed her to do. I mentioned to David that I was going to call the person and tell her I would so appreciate her help. Immediately he responded that I would need to pay her. His response caught me off guard. It was rigid, unbending. It hit me so hard I cried. I did not call to accept the help and feel bad even to now that perhaps I had cheated someone out of a blessing God had intended for her.

Following the unexpected harsh meltdown, I couldn't shake the deflated feeling it left me with. What? I did not feel that I needed to pay her! I labeled myself as a heartless, worthless human being and declared that anyone who thought me to be a nice person must be crazy. Along this appalling journey, I had conquered ills, jumped what I thought to be insurmountable hurdles; but I was weary. I was tired. I was hurt. I was angry. It was too much. This unexpected episode was getting to me. I asked myself if it were worth the fight. Today I was not sure it was.

April 28, 2017: My counselling session with Alice Meyers at Hope Cancer Center went well. I needed it. After much thought and prayer, I had decided to move forward with Taxol chemo treatments. I talked with her about that and she agreed that it was a good choice. Embarrassed and disappointed in myself, I confessed to her about my meltdown. She assured me that it was entirely human, said she was surprised it had not happened sooner. She went on to say that my body had been through a traumatic change. My spiritual, emotional, mental and physical being had been invaded and it was natural to be adversely affected by all this. I would struggle to put the episode out of my mind, but her sympathetic words of wisdom enabled me to move on with renewed courage and determination to press on.

A stop by Smiley's Flea Market to spend a few minutes with Kathy and pick up some Avon warmed my heart. The sun, hidden from my sight, peeped through the clouds that day.

April 29, 2017: Oh, the things we take for granted! I enjoy housekeeping and tried to do a little cleaning. Just being able to sweep, vacuum, dust, clean and cook were blessings I had not realized were so valuable to me. I longed to relish those "chores" again.

April 30, 2017: After church, David and I enjoyed lunch with Derek and Martha at Arby's. Ron and Margaret came for an over-night visit on their way home from a senior retreat in Gatlinburg. They enjoyed the shrimp and grits meal I was able to prepare. My twin was going to make sure I was being true to the promise I had made to myself. As always, time with her was medicine for me.

May 1, 2017: After a simple breakfast, Ron and Margaret headed home. Then David and I ran some errands. I get excited when I think of Wayne and Ashley moving to Bloomington, Illinois. He got the job I mentioned he was interviewing for! Ashley has been given opportunity to continue her present job on-line with limited travel. They will be closer to us. It's 2,318 miles, 33 hours to San Diego vs. 640 miles, 9 hours to Bloomington. Daydreaming about trips there gave me reason to fight for the life I could enjoy with my dear family.

May 2, 2017: I attended Beth Moore's Bible Study at Emma Church and am always inspired by her teaching. Being with my friends that day was also a lift. Kim, a nurse from Home Health Care, came to get my vitals and do a check-up. Dr. Caldwell had scheduled these weekly visits. This check-up went well.

May 3, 2017: I rode with David to Don and Jean Penland's to pick up rock for our new parking area at the entrance to our property. That afternoon, I visited Jean's sister, Sandra, who had suffered a fall and was in rehab following her surgery. She and I enjoyed a meaningful chat regarding the challenges we faced ahead.

May 4, 2017: David and I enjoyed a delightful trip to Knoxville to attend Grace's performance in a band concert. Not only did she perform beautifully, she received two awards at the annual awards presentation. It was hard to believe our first grandchild, our sweet Grace, was 16 going on 17. This visit was another confirmation that I had many reasons to keep fighting for a life that could be so rewarding.

May 5, 2017: My appointment at Hope Cancer Center went well. Brenda flushed my port and said it was working well. Dr. Harkness was pleased with how well I was healing. Dr. Raab felt that I was making the right choice to try the Taxol and assured me that if side effects got rough, the treatment would be stopped immediately. This was a difficult decision for me. I am scheduled for a Taxol training class and blood work on May 10.

On my way home, when I stopped at Ingle's, I met Delores Buchanan who gave me a CD of her wonderful piano playing. This was not a chance meeting; it was another "God wink." She shared her amazing testimony of God's grace in her life, which was exactly what I needed to hear that day.

May 7, 2017: I prepared lunch for Derek and Martha in honor of their anniversary. That afternoon, it felt good to be able to address church bulletins to absentees for the first time this year. I was excited to hear that Alan and Drake may come for a visit. Clinging to every happy moment, I did things to make me feel good. Despite the fact that I had fought the "Red Devil" and won, had come through major surgery and was doing well, I continued to struggle with life. One day I was on top of the world, the next day the world was on top of me. The latest hurdle I was trying to conquer was fear that life was going to be snatched from me and I must make the most of every day. When my counselor said I had come through a traumatic experience that would result in adverse effects on my body and mind, she was not kidding! I had no clue just how profound her prediction would be.

May 8, 2017: Along with eight other women on the cancer battlefield, I attended a class, "Look Good, Feel Good," conducted by The American Cancer Society. We learned how to apply makeup, saw ways to wear scarfs and hats and how best to take care of wigs. I appreciated the free gift – a bag containing $300 worth of excellent beauty products. David and I went to Spectrum and signed up for internet, cable and phone bundle. I made spinach balls (a family favorite). In case you haven't guessed, I'm on top of the world today.

May 10, 2017: I attended the class on Taxol Chemo and had bloodwork done. From research on it, I learned what I had expected to hear. While I was not looking forward to sitting in a chemo chair again, at that moment, I was at peace with my decision, feeling it to be a safety measure I needed to take to avoid recurrence of the cancer.

I met Kathy for lunch at Cracker Barrel. This friend always lifts my spirits and makes me believe I'm gonna make it. It's friends like her that make me think this **road to recovery** is going to be a successful one.

I stopped by Target before my appointment with Dr. Caldwell. This kind doctor exudes God's love and is always a bright spot – especially on a dark day. He recommended the after-surgery Taxol chemo; and I trust this man. His concern for me and care of me are genuine. His recommendation boosted my confidence in my decision.

March 11, 2017: Margaret and Jean came to my house for lunch to celebrate their birthdays. Before these two forever friends left, they dusted and vacuumed my house. Kim, the healthcare nurse came for her weekly visit, which went well. Am I blessed or what?

May 12, 2017: Marsha Honeycutt (a friend who had attended our church at Emma and still stayed in touch) treated me to breakfast at Duncan Donuts. I stopped by Ingles to pick up a few groceries on my way home.

May 13, 2017: David and I joined our church family at Mills River Restaurant for an outing. Then he and I shopped at Big Lots and Target to get some things for the coming week.

May 14, 2017: After church, David and I enjoyed chicken at Bojangles. When we got home, I prepared for Alan and Drake's visit, addressed church bulletins to absentees and watched a Hallmark movie – enjoying a relaxing day.

What a treat when Alan and Drake arrived. Our little guy was so excited to present me with a Wonder Woman Balloon for Mother's Day and snuggle with me on the couch. I had purchased the Power Rangers gown I'm wearing in the children's department as I knew Drake would like it; and I was right.

A Moment to Remember ~ Grandma and Drake

My excited grandson exclaimed, “Grandma, that is the prettiest dress I have ever seen you wear.”

As special as my family had made this day for me, I still fought a feeling of sadness. This was Mother’s Day. I was missing my mother, who had been gone almost four years.

7

In the Chair Again

May 15, 2017: What was I doing here? My cancer was gone; I had proof of that! Why was I sitting in a chemo chair again? Even though I had come to grips with my decision and felt peace about it, my mind still played tricks on me from time to time. It's good at doing that. Friends and family had expressed their opinions; but assured me the decision was mine and that whatever it was, they would stand with me. I asked myself two questions and pondered them days on end.

- If the cancer recurs, could I have prevented it if I had taken the treatment?
- If I take the treatment and the cancer recurs, why did I put myself through this?

I was riding a roller coaster, that ride at the amusement park that reaches great heights and suddenly takes great plunges. When I sat down in that chair, it made a sudden plunge; but I was on for the ride and couldn't ask the attendant to stop the machine so I held on tight. Thankfully, the treatment went well – no complications and no reactions.

Taxol did not require the Neulasta pro-on-body injector. That was the good news I needed. Cancer sisters who had taken this journey were honest to say there would be side effects but assured me this treatment was not as fierce as the "Red Devil." I was "on the road again" (I mean **in the chair again**). As a reward for my accomplishment, David and I stopped on the way home for a Celebrity hotdog. We, along with many others, believe it to be the best hotdog in the South.

May 16, 2017: During her weekly visit, the home health care nurse explained some of the side effects Taxol might have: Fatigue, loss of hair, weight loss and mouth sores.

May 17-18, 2017: David and I dined at Arby's with Alan and Drake. We shopped at Target before we met Roland and Katrina for supper at Cheddar's. Alan and Drake enjoyed spending time with them. Cold Stone ice cream topped off our great evening.

Time with family (priceless)

May 19-20, 2017: Our precious Knoxville family came for the weekend. On Saturday we enjoyed a ride to Chimney Rock and Lake Lure, one of our favorite spots. The trip also included one of our favorite menus: Kentucky Fried Chicken, potato wedges, corn on the cob, green beans and watermelon.

Life doesn't get much better than "chicken by the sea" (I mean by a lake). What was more special was that I had temporarily come back into the "season of taste." Jamie and Grace had to return to Knoxville for another band concert; but DJ, John and Luke were able to stay through the weekend.

Hand in hand, David and I took another walk around the lake where we had walked many times through the years, even when our sons were toddlers. Reflecting on special memories, the surroundings were even more beautiful. I was thankful to be making another memory with my family, alive, clinging tight to this moment. After our walk, I found a cute pink hat (and sighed). Taxol would take away what little hair had grown back.

David and Martha – Another walk to remember

May 22, 2017: My second Taxol treatment went well and I was permitted to go to Southport. May 29 was Memorial Day, so I would skip treatment that day.

May 24, 2017: Ben Adair, David's uncle, died. We were thankful to have attended their 70th anniversary celebration in February, not realizing it would be our last time to see him here. We look forward to meeting him on the other side.

May 26, 2017: We went to Fayetteville to attend Uncle Ben's bittersweet home-going and joined the family for a buffet meal prepared by ladies of the church following the service. Seeing the Bass extended family again was special. They thought I looked great for all I had been through and promised their continued prayers. From there we went to the grave site of David's parents, Kirby and Katie. Then we enjoyed a visit with my brother Doyle and his wife Judy.

June 1, 2017: Doyle and Judy were on their way to their place in Topsail and invited us to meet them in Wilmington. They treated Alan, Drake, David and me to a meal at Elijah's on the waterfront (one of our favorite dining spots). Our walk on the Boardwalk was relaxing and fun.

June 2, 2017: David and I left Southport midday and spent time in Concord with Ron and Margaret before we went to Christy's daughter, Peyton's home-school graduation party.

June 3, 2017: I enjoyed a Wood Family Reunion in Bryson City. Seeing Aunt Oleta, Hazel, Ruth and Judy was lots of fun. I shared my testimony of God's faithfulness through my difficult cancer journey as I ate with cousins Dawn, Angie and Amy. At the same time, the gathering was sad as so many were missing – waiting for us on the other side.

June 5, 2017: I had my third Taxol treatment. The Benadryl given prior to the treatment made me sleepy. When I got home, I laid down at 5:40 p.m. and woke up at 8:44 p.m. David laughed when I walked out of the bedroom and asked what he wanted for breakfast, reminding him that I needed to get to Bible study at 10:00 a.m. Guess I needed that extended rest but it was hard to go back to sleep that night. I am going to ask how much Benadryl they gave me. Now that I am doing better, three-hour naps don't work well in my schedule. I did manage to stay awake the next day for the Bible study. Beth Moore is always inspiring. So far, so good, no raging side effects.

June 7, 2017: David and I enjoyed our favorite garden omelet at I-Hop with Dave and Linda Barbour. Thankfully, the Taxol has still not kicked me down like the "Red Devil" did.

If she were still here, Mother would have celebrated her 93rd birthday today. She's celebrating in a land of total bliss where she will be forever young. As much as I miss her, I would not call her back to the world where there is so much pain. Being the caring, compassionate person she was, this journey I am taking would have been difficult for her.

June 8, 2017: We enjoyed a meal at Cheddar's with Roland, Katrinia, Jason and Sharon. Instead of my usual order for spinach dip with chips, I got a burger. No chemo mouth: I could taste it; was it ever so good! We enjoyed shopping at Barnes and Nobel after we ate. We had a nice weekend. I was able to help with the yard sale at Emma. Things I used to take for granted are special now. Everything has meaning for me.

June 12, 2017: Before my fourth Taxol treatment, I met with Dr. Raab. She commended me for my fortitude and perseverance, thankful that Taxol's side effects had been of little consequence and glad to hear that I was beginning to enjoy life again. She was not the only one thankful for all that!

June 13, 2017: After Bible study, I went with David for his annual physical to the VA Medical Center. Going there always brings back memories I made during my 27 years of employment (some good – some bad). I said hi to friends and co-workers while he waited for lab work. I was too tired to attend the healing service as planned but did not chide myself for it. One lesson I have learned is to listen to my body. I'm getting better at it. When my body says, " I need rest," I rest.

June 14, 2017: Today was a landmark on this journey. I had an appointment at Pink Regalia to be fitted for my prosthetic bra. At my age, I chose this over reconstructive surgery. Each lady who has helped me through this strange new experience, has been compassionate and put me at ease, making the ordeal as pleasant as possible. The bras are nice, expensive. Since this is not considered "cosmetic" (as some surgeries are), I have good insurance that entirely covers them.

Following that appointment, I met Kathy Stepp for lunch. She called our meeting "Celebrate New Boob Day." This new bra does help make me feel "whole" again. The matching look means more than I could have imagined. My sweet friend and I had some good laughs over this reality. I jumped an awkward hurdle today, one that I could be proud of, one that brought a smile all the way from my heart to my face.

June 15, 2017: My appointment at Hope Cancer Center with Alice went well but was thought provoking. Full of love and compassion, she has been a rock for me to run to in scary, unfamiliar territory. She asked me what was the hardest thing to deal with right now. I told her it was fear that the cancer would recur. She said that was totally understandable. She went on to say when those fears torment me, to remind myself that God has brought me this far and would never leave me.

Then she took a surprising approach that made me take a different look at all of this. She asked how strong my faith was if the cancer did come back and God chose to heal me through death. "Are you afraid to die?" She lovingly asked.

How do you answer a question like that? It wasn't hard for me. I had already asked it of myself. "No." I said, "With everything in me, I want to live. I don't want to leave my family, knowing how much my death would hurt them. I enjoy our times together: Playing with the younger 'grands,' having meaningful conversations with the older ones, building fires in the chiminea, preparing meals with my sons, walking on the beach at sunset, the 'us' time David and I have, simple things like trips to Bojangles or Lowe's. It doesn't take a lot to make me happy. I love life but I'm not afraid to die. Many on the other side are waiting to welcome me home. As much as I enjoy life here, I will leave this world for a better place."

June 16, 2017: When I returned from my counseling session, chemo fatigue wiped me out – my first bad Taxol day. I made hamburgers for supper and sat down to watch a movie, fell asleep in the recliner and went to bed at 7:30 p.m. After over 14 hours of sleep, I woke up at 9:30 a.m. That's what chemo fatigue did to me. After the rest, David and I went to Bojangles for breakfast. I came home, cleaned windows, fixed fish for supper and burned wood in the chimenea. Once I had gotten the needed rest, I was ready to hit the chores again. You can only keep me down so long.

June 18, 2017: On Father's Day we rode over to Scaly Mountain to see improvements renters had made on Mom and Dad's little house on the hill. The couple had planned to purchase the property and had already started making changes. This situation was awkward as they should have made those changes only after the purchase! Advising us that they were making them would have been appropriate. Walls had been taken down. Bunk beds had been built into a wall, making one of the guest bedrooms much smaller. We reminded them that according to the contract, they were supposed to advise us of changes. They said they were getting it like they wanted it for themselves, so we did not pursue the matter at that time.

We enjoyed time with Uncle Emmit and Aunt Joyce. As I watched him, he reminded me of his brother, my dad. In declining health, he hardly spoke a word during our visit.

June 19, 2017: The fifth Taxol treatment went well. However, while I was burning wood in the chimenea after I got home, I broke a fingernail off to the quick. One of the side effects of this drug is loss of fingernails and toenails. This simple yet painful incident plunged me again into the depths of despair (I think I mentioned that I don't like roller coasters).

June 20, 2017: Margaret Roberts treated me to lunch at Olive Garden. Spending time with a special friend made me feel better.

June 21-25, 2017: I took home-made tomato soup to the UMC ladies' meeting. Afterward, Cathy Jackaway cleaned my house, brightened my day. After helping with the summer feeding program at Emma Thursday and organizing photos for our up-coming 50th anniversary, chemo fatigue returned and I took it easy. Sunday several of the Basses met us at Golden Corral to celebrate the recent or upcoming birthdays of David, Ellon, Stan, Kenneth and Katrina.

June 26, 2017: Taxol treatment went well. I was given permission to go to Southport and skip my next treatment so the Bass family could enjoy our annual fourth of July vacation there. Having Margaret and Ron at their place during this time made being there more special. They celebrated David's 74th birthday with us at Fifty Fifth, a new restaurant on Oak Island.

8

Faith, Fun, Friends and Family

July 1-7, 2017: Alan, Drake, David and I headed to Myrtle Beach with a stop at Matthews Pancake House in Little River for lunch. The text came from the resort that our condo was ready. We checked in before 2:00 p.m. We met the K-town family at Chesapeake Restaurant for dinner and enjoyed board games back at the condo. The plan to spend the vacation at Myrtle Beach was my family's idea to let me know how much they cared for me and didn't want me to spend time working at our house in Southport during vacation week. The lovely four-bedroom condo filled with laughter and love was the best medicine ever.

We enjoyed an awesome week of fun, food, faith and family. Family members prepared a delicious breakfast every morning. We dined at several different restaurants, including Calabash where we spent time at St. Nick Nack's and picked up our favorite flavors of fudge. One day we rode back to Southport to dine at the Frying Pan and get Drake back to Holly. We enjoyed ice cream at Spike's. Back at the condo, we did our own thing. Grace and I read while others watched a movie. With a day filled with so much fun, it was another 1:00 a.m. bedtime.

Our times out on the beach were nice. The guys had put up an umbrella for me even before I walked out to enjoy these times of relaxation. Margaret and Ron joined us one day. She brought her famous "Huntersville hamburgers."

I had been back in the chair five times while Taxol was forced through my veins. God had brought me through so much; and I had to trust Him to continue to be with me every step of this scary journey. As I sat on a balcony looking out over the vast endless sea, surrounded by love, I realized there could be no better healing than faith and family. It was so good not to have chemo this week. I felt "almost normal."

July 8, 2017: After a delightful breakfast at Hoskins, the K-town family headed West. Alan, David and I headed to Southport. While the guys unloaded the car, I put things away and started preparing for our return to Asheville.

July 9, 2017: We stopped at K&W in Asheboro for lunch and arrived back in Asheville. Even the tall grass did not dim our high spirits. David just got out the mower.

July 10, 2017: My oncology appointment went well today. Dr. Raab was impressed by how well I was doing. She gave me a thorough exam and discussed "signs to watch for" in case cancer recurs: Check regularly and carefully for any lumps in left breast or even mastectomy site. Beware of recurring/lingering headaches, excessive coughing, back or lower abdominal pain. My prayer is that I never feel any of these.

Chemo treatment number seven went well. The Benadryl did its thing and I had a two-and-a-half-hour nap when I got home. The busy week included Bible study, cleaning house, helping with Emma's project to feed the children in the community. I continued to play the role of Martha in what was becoming my busy world, while keeping a "Mary heart."

I love the book, *Having a Mary Heart in a Martha World*, by Joanna Weaver. This book was a gift given to me by guests I served at the Cove. When guests at the Cove saw my name, they would comment, "We have the right person as our server." I would respond that I was thankful to have a "Martha heart" (a busy servant heart); but that I strive to have a "Mary Heart" (a heart that longs to spend time with the Lord in prayer and devotion). The busyness of life has made that a challenge.

July 14, 2017: Margaret and Ron arrived mid-afternoon following another visit to their favorite house, the Biltmore Estate. After supper, we went to Mast General Store in downtown Asheville and shopped at Hamrick's where we found good bargains, making it a profitable venture. We made cookies for Margaret to take to Uncle Emmit as they were headed to Scaly Mountain the next day.

July 16, 2017: After church, we had home-made chicken noodle soup. I rested then addressed bulletins to absentees. At 2:30 p.m. I went to work at the Cove. This was a red letter day as it was my first day of work in 2017. My co-workers welcomed me with open arms. Margaret Roberts saw to it that this was a pleasant experience. As my co-worker that day, she also saw to it that I did not overdo it!

July 17, 2017: My eighth chemo treatment was another good one; and again, we headed to Southport. When we arrived we found Alan all packed and ready for his trip to San Diego.

July 18, 2017: Holly brought Drake over and he was so excited about the trip. After breakfast at Bojangles, we got them to the Wilmington airport in plenty of time for their flight. David and I stopped at Sam's and Walmart in Wilmington. What a pleasant surprise when we got back home to find that Ron and Margaret had come to Southport to surprise me. That twin of mine is full of surprises that always brighten my world.

That week we enjoyed being together: "Twin talk," joint meals, relaxing on the bay, milkshakes at Spikes, time in the Christmas Shop. Life is good.

But then, life is hard. I am concerned about Diane, David's cousin. She is in the hospital at Myrtle Beach, fighting her battle with lung cancer.

July 21, 2017: Margaret and I got ready for a yard sale we were planning for today. Big mistake! Things don't always work out as you had hoped. To say the yard sale was unsuccessful would be the understatement of the year. Very few customers came; and those who did only looked. We closed up shop early and took some things to a consignment shop. The proprietor took some of the things but not as many as we had hoped he would. You just can't win 'em all and you certainly can't make a living on yard sales.

July 22, 2017: All too soon, Margaret and Ron were headed home to Concord. Since the line to eat at Bojangles (first choice) was long, we ate at McDonald's with them on their way out.

July 23, 2017: David and I went to Bayboro to visit Margaret White and her husband Frankie. The warm welcome included Frankie's fried fresh flounder he had caught on Saturday, fries, slaw, croissants, and peach cobbler. Frankie's son Greg and his wife Paula joined us. She had brought chicken, baked beans and mac and cheese. We enjoyed a feast!

It was nice to be with this dear friend again. Margaret and I met 43 years ago while working at VA Medical Center and declared friendship for life. We sat on the porch, looking out over the beautiful water and caught up on each other's life, our children, health concerns.... We recalled special memories we had made through the years. Margaret's husband, Don, had died; and I was thankful God had sent Frankie into her life. Their beautiful home at River's Edge Family Campground was a postcard setting, a tranquil paradise.

July 24, 2017: Frankie drove us to Oriental and other interesting sites in the area we had never seen. I was grateful that Dr. Raab had allowed me to skip another chemo treatment, giving us opportunity for this better-than-ever imagined time with friends. My initial decision to take additional treatment for preventive measures was made with the stipulation that I would be allowed to postpone treatments now and then.

July 25, 2017: We got the word that Diane, David's cousin I had been concerned about, had left for heaven. She had fought her cancer battle with courage for several years. Now her pain was over. We would attend her memorial service in Fayetteville on our way home to Asheville.

July 26, 2017: I freshened up the house. While we got a heavy rain, I watched a couple of Christmas movies. Christmas in July is also good medicine for this cancer patient.

July 27, 2017: I took some of the things Margaret and I had left from our yard sale to Three Sisters Consignment shop. The kind lady there was happy to accept some of our things.

July 28, 2017: Devastated and overcome with grief, my precious friend Kathy Stepp called to say her twin, Kathleen, had died in her sleep. I felt so sad for her. Finding words that would comfort her was difficult. I could not imagine her pain; so I did the only thing I could; I cried with her.

July 29, 2017: While David waded in the waves, I sat in a beach chair and read *Just Right.* I could not believe our time in Southport was ending; it had passed so fast. Even though we missed Alan and Drake, we enjoyed our "us" time.

July 30, 2017: After attending Little River UMC, we enjoyed lunch at Matthews. Then we picked our guys up at the airport in Wilmington. We enjoyed hearing about their awesome trip to San Diego.

July 31, 2017: We left Southport to attend Diane's celebration of life. The graveside service was so sad. The ceremony of loved ones and friends throwing a hand full of dirt on the coffin or urn of one deceased symbolizes that the deceased has returned to the earth from where he/she came. This ritual was difficult for Diane's mother. She was only able to accomplish it as she was held up by her sons. I will never get out of my mind the crushing memory of dear Aunt Annos and her trembling hands as she attempted to throw dirt on the body of her precious daughter, who had preceded her in death. The scene was heartbreaking. I struggled with deep sadness on our trip home, fighting tears of grief and loss.

When we arrived home in Asheville, the bright spot in my day came. Wayne and Ashley called with the most wonderful news we could have gotten. They informed us that another little Bass was on the way, expected to arrive on March 22, 2018. I have loved being a grandmother since the day our precious Grace gave me a new name; and I knew the depth of the meaning of the word "grand." Every time we welcomed a new grandchild into the world, it became one of the most special days in our lives. The news of another grandchild on the way gave me renewed hope, strength, courage and a greater purpose to fight this perplexing battle and win! I looked forward to meeting this new little Bass that was coming to join our family.

August 1, 2017: I had my treatment on Tuesday this week. The home health nurse came for her scheduled visit that afternoon and advised me that chemo fatigue was expected to increase. My nap lasted three hours after she left; but I slept very little that night. I had to find a way to change this routine. While it was not nearly as harsh as the "Red Devil," the fatigue was becoming a real issue.

August 2, 2017: Dr. Sarah Cash, the dermatologist, removed an annoying mole from my upper arm. She did not suspect anything bad; but it would be biopsied just to be sure. What I loved about this sweet doctor was that she had moved to Asheville from Concord and was once my twin's doctor, who came highly recommended.

After my appointment with Dr. Cash, I came by Emma Church to help set up for Saturday's upcoming yard sale. My busy week continued.

August 3, 2017: I worked with Margaret Roberts again at the Cove. Everyone seemed delighted to see me. I did my share of work but being there was actually relaxing for me. It was a withdrawal from arduous days I had endured and felt more like fun than work.

August 4, 2017: Workers from Lowes continued to install new windows on our round house. They were looking good. Seeing this home improvement that we had longed to have done was an uplift.

Wayne and Ashley left San Diego, California heading to Bloomington, Illinois to begin their new life there. We are so proud of our Wayne who will begin his position as Professor of Humanities at Heartland Community College.

David and I joined Don, Jean, Frankie and Margaret at Tommy's in Weaverville (another favorite meet-to-eat place). We enjoyed the fun, food and fellowship. Moments with friends like these are some of life's best gifts.

August 5, 2017: Fifty years ago today on a pier at Carolina Beach, David asked me to be his wife. I'm glad I said yes. This was the correct answer. We are looking forward to our Golden Wedding Anniversary Celebration December 31.

Working at the Emma yard sale and spending time with my church family was fun. But as Linda had warned, chemo fatigue was not getting any better; it was getting worse. I relaxed and watched two Hallmark movies when I got home.

August 6, 2017: After church and lunch, I watched a Hallmark movie and addressed bulletins to absentees.

At 4:30 p.m. I went to work at the Cove and enjoyed another experience with friends and coworkers, another “get away” I needed.

Unfortunately, when Wayne and Ashley arrived in Bloomington, the house they had rented nowhere resembled the beautiful little house they had seen online. What they entered was a total mess. Upon contacting the landlord, he promised to have it cleaned.

August 7, 2017: With the new windows in, we were not able to put up blinds yet; so David helped me hang some temporary curtains in our bedroom.

August 8, 2017: My Taxol treatment went well. I forced myself to stay awake so I would be able to sleep tonight. We continued to work on getting up curtains to cover the windows.

Wayne and Ashley’s house had gotten cleaned. We were thankful they had a safe trip to their new place and even more grateful that our sweet Ashley’s pregnancy was going well.

August 9, 2017: David and I met James, Venetia and Roland at Nara’s. Because Katrina had hurt her back, she was not able to join us; and I missed her. Roland brought us fresh green beans and corn; and I enjoyed making a garden supper the following day.

August 13, 2017: For my Sunday routine, after church I watched a Hallmark movie and addressed bulletins for absentees. At 3:00 p.m. I found myself back at the Cove (my ‘hide away”) where I enjoyed another good shift.

August 14, 2017: Back at the Cove again, I got the devastating news that Coleen, a coworker had been told she had lung cancer. Hearing that brought back the dreadful memory of that day in Santa Barbara when the “C” diagnosis had been pronounced to me, a moment I will never forget.

Shortly after I got home, our dear DJ arrived to go with me to my chemo treatment the following day.

August 15, 2017: After breakfast at I-Hop, David went to Charlotte to be with Ellon, his sister, who was having surgery that day. Just as I knew they would, everyone in the chemo lab loved DJ. Alice, my counselor, came in the lab while we were there. She told him she didn't know how I did it but that I had more energy than she did. I warned my son that I was no fun after chemo as it zonked me out. Benadryl kicked in quickly that day and I slept over four hours. Roland and David had a good visit with Ellon. She came through the surgery like the trooper that she is. My precious son left me a note, thanking me for being his "Wonder Woman Mom." For some reason, this injection left me extremely fatigued; and I did very little that week other than rest. "Wonder Woman" would not be the description I would have given myself. A more fitting title in my opinion would have been "Resting Rooster."

August 18, 2017: David and I enjoyed breakfast with Dave and Linda Barbour at Five Points. Don Penland stopped by to speak to us while we were there. When we left the restaurant, we learned that he had paid for our meal -- a thoughtful gesture from a thoughtful friend! By the end of the week, chemo fatigue had hit so hard it was scary. Perhaps I had hit more buttons than I realized; so I rested.

August 20, 2017: Roland and Katrinia came over and cooked their famous shrimp and fish feast for us. Being with them is always a treat; but unfortunately, the food was not. Due to the dreaded chemo-mouth that had returned, what would have been delicious and enjoyable tasted bitter to me.

August 21, 2017: During my office visit, Dr. Raab said she was so impressed with my progress. The news she shared with me was even better than her compliments. She reminded me that tomorrow would be my last Taxol treatment. I wanted to do an Indian dance; but I was too tired. I simply smiled and with every ounce of enthusiasm I could muster, thanked her for this great update.

August 22, 2017: Exactly eight months ago today, on December 22, 2016, I discovered a lump in my breast. Today I am finishing my last chemo treatment.

Last Day of Chemo

When that last infusion was completed, nurses in the chemo lab, who had been good to me through every treatment, presented me with a certificate of completion while they blew bubbles into the air and applauded my accomplishments. These compassionate, caring folks had become dear friends. I would never forget them.

Along with the box of cookies I had baked for them, I had written a note of thanks to them for taking such good care of me during the most difficult chapter of my life. I promised to keep in touch and to stop by and see them when I returned to the oncologist for my three-month follow-ups. With tears in their eyes, they hugged me and said to please come by.

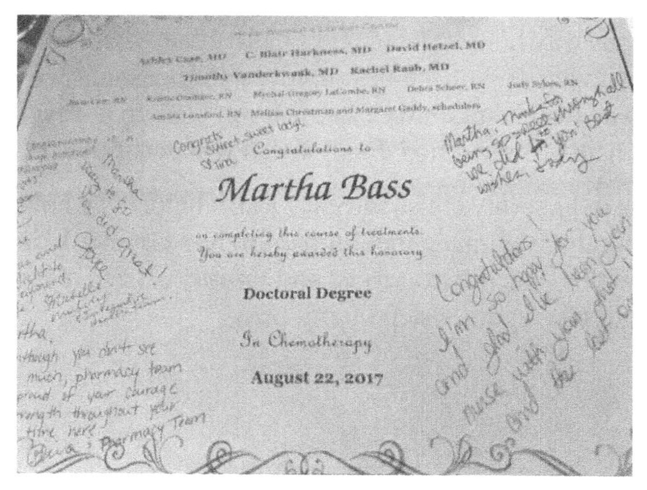

Certificate of Completion

Janet, my nurse navigator, gave me information relative to support groups for cancer survivors and encouraged me to get involved. She felt that doing so would be helpful.

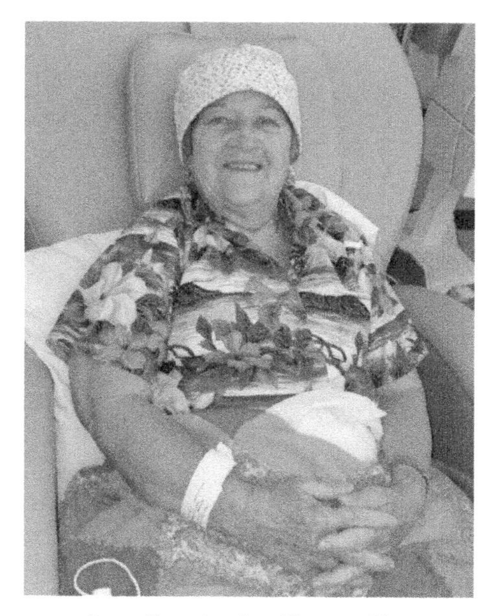

Last Day in the Chemo Chair

On our way home, David and I enjoyed another Celebrity hotdog. Having one of the best hotdogs in the South was the perfect way to celebrate! My taste was not back to normal; but I was so happy, I imagined that it tasted wonderful!

How did I survive this journey? **Faith** helped me hold on; **Fun** along the way made the journey more bearable; **Friends** walked with me on difficult days; and **Family** carried me when I could not take another step on my own.

9

What Is Next?

August 23, 2017: Anyone who knows me well knows I enjoy rearranging furniture every year or so. I actually have means of moving it and can do much of it myself. Nothing stays the same way for very long. But to ask David to help me rearrange the furniture in the living room today was not a good request to make. The couch was extremely heavy and put a strain on his back. I loved the new look of the room; but the memory of the ordeal plunged me once again into the depths of gloom, despair and agony.

I had finished chemo; and I was supposed to be rejoicing. Instead I was beating Martha up again, wondering why God would have chosen to heal this worthless human being. Why had He just not let me die? David would certainly have a much better life without a wife and all the "Honey Dos" she demands and he encounters. I was having a miserable day. God said He would not put more on us than we could bear; and I really needed Him to lift me out of the pits.

As Patsy Clairmont, the famous author and comedian says, "God, this is hard, really hard. You're not looking!"

God sent a ray of sunshine when I heard from Wayne and Ashley that they were enjoying their new life in Bloomington with a teaching position where he is deeply appreciated.

August 24, 2017: A large picture hanging over the television downstairs needed to be hung a little higher; so I took it down for David to rehang. As I was removing it from the wall, it fell out of the frame (heavy sigh).

As if this dilemma were not enough to send me over the edge, I went out to help David burn wood in the chimenea and was stung by fire ants on my chest near my port cath. It felt like my chest was on fire. "Dear God in heaven," I silently screamed, "Please assure me that this is not **what is next** for me. It has got to get better. I can't do this!"

August 28, 2017: My visit with Alice Myer, my dear counselor, was the lift I needed. She told me my question, "Where do I go from here (**what is next**)?" was the most normal question any person in my circumstance could ask. She warned me that I would face days of uncertainty, moments of fear and doubt, and perhaps even bouts of crying, trying desperately to deal with the unknown. She could not answer my $64,000 question. She could only assure me it was a normal one. Just knowing that it was normal made the load seem a little bit lighter.

August 29, 2017: The Beth Moore Bible study at Emma from the book of Daniel was so uplifting. From there I went by the State Employees' Credit Union to make a deposit. I left my phone there and had to go back to get it. I am beginning to wonder if the overload of trying to figure all this out includes increased absent-mindedness (aka chemo-brain)?

August 30, 2017: This was the best day yet in this new normal. How uplifting it was to visit our Knoxville family in their new home. We were en route to Bloomington.

September 1, 2017: My counselor told me this traveling plan was a great way to celebrate. We toured Heartland Community College where Dr. Wayne Bass is a professor, teaching humanities and religious studies. We missed seeing Ashley who was away on an out-of-town work assignment.

We were delighted to see the place Wayne now called home and had come to love in such a short time. He is a gifted teacher and loves what he does. That's what matters.

David and Martha
Downtown Chicago, Lake Michigan

September 2-7, 2017: Our first trip to the Windy City of Chicago was amazing. We were fascinated with its many sites. Following special time with our K-town family and the professor in Bloomington, we arrived safely home with heads and hearts full of memories to treasure.

September 13, 2017: Mary Beth, another "cancer sister," who had travelled this road before me, texted me about Kelly Mehler, her friend who had just been diagnosed with breast cancer. I called Kelly to assure her of my prayers and tell her I hoped I could be a help to her on the dreadful journey on which she was about to embark. Even though I had not been privileged to meet this precious lady from California in person, she and I connected immediately as friends.

September 27, 2017: Cathy Jackaway came to clean the house; having her come was a blessing. Someone from Hope Cancer Center called to ask if I would be willing to do an interview for an article in the *Asheville Citizen Times*, highlighting details of my cancer story. I understood from her explanation that two patients were chosen each year during October (breast cancer month). The vote that I be one of those patients was unanimous. What an honor!

September 28, 2017: My interview scheduled with the writer from *Asheville Citizens Times* was postponed due to a family illness. She said she would call the next day.

Jean Penland's cousin, JoAnn Shepherd, died today just three weeks after she learned she had cancer! Hearing that another one had died of cancer broke my heart. And the question, What will my outcome be?" screamed in my head.

September 29, 2017: True to her word, the lady who was going to interview me called the following morning. The interview lasted just over an hour. I tried to be as accurate as possible with details of my story and looked forward to seeing it in print.

My follow-up appointment with Dr. Condra, radiologist, went well. I was thankful to learn that I do not have to take radiation treatments. Due to the size of my tumor, it was borderline as to whether I needed it or not. I chose NOT to take the treatments.

October 3, 2017: My appointment with Dr. Raab went well. She said I was doing great. I am scheduled to see her again on January 9, 2018, following my mammogram. My port is booked to be taken out on October 31. When I left Hope Cancer Center, I went to Amanda's beauty salon and left my wig to get a pink stripe for breast cancer awareness month.

Tonight, I attended my first cancer support group along with 12 others who had taken their cancer journey. To hear their stories was heart-wrenching, overwhelming.

October 24, 2017: I attended the cancer support group meeting and did the Yoga class at the beginning of the session. Tonight's topics were Emotions and Coping. That night, Ann, a member of the group, shared with us that her cancer was back. Listening to her update, as tears dripped from her face, was an emotional time for class members who had come to love her.

On the way home, how exciting to learn that Wayne and Ashley's baby is a girl. That news put me on cloud nine! Wayne has wanted to be a dad for so long; and he will be a great one!

October 31, 2017: What a **treat** on Halloween to get my port taken out. The numbing was the worst part of the procedure. It felt like a swarm of bees landed on my chest and attacked it viciously Getting rid of this sometimes bothersome nine-month companion was a blessing.

My last support group meeting was special. Chaplain of the cancer center and a medical oncologist spoke. They asked each of us questions. Everyone participated in the discussion, one of the things I've enjoyed most in this group setting.

November 1, 2017: I am getting compliments on the article on my cancer story that was published in the *Asheville Citizen's Times.* Other than a few misquotes from the interview, it was a good write-up.

November 2, 2017: We had planned another trip to Knoxville to hear Luke in his 6th grade band concert. The aftermath of my port removal was more uncomfortable than I had expected. The area was very sore and I did not feel like taking the ride. As disappointing as my decision was, once again, I listened to my body and did what I needed to do.

November 5, 2017: I felt a tightness in my upper chest that made my shoulders and neck ache constantly. This new pain was stressing me out. Perhaps it was a muscle cramp or spasm brought on from removal of the port, something I would discuss with Rachel, the nurse practitioner, at the survivorship meeting on Tuesday.

November 7, 2017: I attended the survivorship meeting and heard ideas for staying healthy in hopes of preventing cancer from recurring. As I suspected, Rachel felt that the new pain in my neck and shoulders could be muscle spasms from removal of the port.

November 8-15, 2017: David and I went to Concord. Margaret and I shopped for my dress for our 50th anniversary celebration. We found the perfect one for me at Ross. This store chain already has amazing prices. This dress was on sale. And even its total price – $17.11 – had significance. The material for my wedding dress, which my mother had made in 1967, cost $17.

We went from Concord to Southport. During our week there, Alan and Drake found shirts and pants for the upcoming 50th anniversary celebration; and David found his new black suit. I shopped for decorations for the occasion.

November 20-24, 2017: I delivered Christmas cards and 50th anniversary invitations to Hope Cancer Center and had another Celebrity hotdog with David. Alan and Drake arrived from Southport. We enjoyed a Thanksgiving get-together with them and the K-town family. Then we went to Emma Church to check out the fellowship hall for detailed planning of the upcoming 50th celebration.

December 1-8, 2017: Roland and Katrinia came to the house and we headed to Jacksonville, Florida where we would take a cruise as part of our 50th anniversary celebration. James, Venetia and their friend Cindy met us in Jacksonville where we spent the night.

We boarded the Magic Carnival at 12:20 p.m. the following day. After a delicious lunch, we went to our room with a window view. Dinner in the main dining room was delicious. Our first cruise port was Amber Cove in Dominican Republic. After another delectable meal in the Northern Lights dining room, we attended a great show. Roland and Katrinia celebrated their 21st anniversary this week. We enjoyed more meals and more sites. The cruise went by so quickly; but we had lots of fun. I was happy to be cancer-free, happy to be alive! We had enjoyed sunny days on the cruise – what a contrast to arrive home in Asheville to 11 inches of snow.

December 11-13, 2017: My appointment with Dr. Caldwell went great. He was proud of my good blood pressure reading. We went to Knoxville for Luke's 6th grade band concert. I was happy to be able to attend this one. Jamie had prepared a delicious meal for us; and after the concert, we enjoyed banana splits. As I said, it doesn't take a lot to make me happy. Simple things in life were becoming even more amazing. Every day was a gift, "my present."

December 15-17, 2017: I had lunch with Kathy and got some things from her flea market for the 50th celebration. She was grieving the death of her twin and feeling great concern for her husband who was in poor health. My heart ached for her and I wished there were something I could do to lighten my friend's load.

After lunch with Margaret Roberts, I asked David to check a place on my lower back that was itching really bad. We both cringed. I called Dr. Caldwell's office and spoke with the on-call doctor regarding my symptoms. She phoned in a prescription for me. Unfortunately, I did not make it to CVS Pharmacy before they closed. I begged God to help me! Having had shingles about five years ago, I knew they had returned and wanted to get ahead of them before they got a hold on me! I was able to get my prescription on Sunday; and thankfully, the medicine helped them heal. I have heard that stress can cause shingles. Stress had been my way of life for eight months. Once again, I had proved what is said by many to be true.

Martha with Dr. Caldwell and Sabrina

December 22, 2017: One year ago today I found a lump in my right breast. The past year seems like a nightmare but it was reality. I survived chemo, surgery and jumped many hurdles. The love of friends and family and God's faithfulness brought me through. I am cancer-free!

December 25, 2017: On Christmas day, we stopped by Ron and Margaret's on our way home to Asheville. After we enjoyed "Huntersville hamburgers," David and I sat on the couch to visit. Margaret brought out a pink scrapbook. She handed it to me and said, "This is something Christy and I made for you." All year she had been taking pictures; but I had no idea what she was doing. She and Christy had put hours into creating my story. Tears dripped from my face as I looked through my journey, detailed in chronological order with pictures and inspiring captions.

I still get it out now and then and look through it, grateful for the lessons I learned on this journey. I also take it with me when I am invited to share my story in public settings. While seeing its contents are painful, it is also a gift I will treasure forever. It was created with so much love and is another confirmation that I am a survivor.

The Scrapbook

December 26-29, 2017: After breakfast with Jean, Don, Margaret and Frankie at Cracker Barrel, we came home and prepared for the arrival of Alan, Drake, Wayne and Ashley. The Illinois family arrived just before midnight. Over the next few days, we enjoyed time with our precious family and Chef Wayne's cooking. We had our post-Christmas feast with the K-town family. And in keeping with the family tradition, we had a blast opening gifts.

December 30, 2017: We spent time at Emma Church decorating for the celebration. Jamie and Grace spent the day baking. Grace created beautiful unique cupcakes, the most delicious I have ever seen/tasted. That night we surprised Wayne and Ashley with a baby shower. It was great to have Ron and Margaret with us. Reed, Jenn and Sawyer were visiting from California. We get to see them so seldom, having them here was icing on the cake. It turned out to be a special family reunion.

10

Celebrating Survival and Fifty Golden Years

Everyone has a story to tell. Perhaps someday you will write yours and say, "My story is not over, I am a survivor."

In January 2017 I realized what a significant year it was: David and I would celebrate our 50th wedding anniversary on December 31, the last day of the year. But many times, I asked myself, "Will I be here to celebrate with him? Will I survive this cancer?"

When I made reference to this milestone, Dr. Harkness, my surgeon, his nurse, Brenda, Dr. Raab, my oncologist, and other members of my health care team at Hope Cancer Center assured me they would do everything they could to help make sure I was here to celebrate this awesome event. Thanks to the health care team and most of all to God for so many answered prayers. I was cancer free on December 31.

Our three sons, daughters-in-love and grandchildren planned one of the most meaningful celebrations I have ever attended. At Emma United Methodist Church, where David and I had attended for years, several gathered to celebrate 50 years of love, life and laughter, mixed with the pain and difficulties that only made them stronger.

As David and I entered the sanctuary, we were amazed to see family, church family, friends, co-workers, neighbors and medical staff smiling at us. To begin the program, our nephew, Reed, prayed a beautiful prayer, thanking God for the example of love we had maintained and shared with others for 50 years.

David and Martha Bass
50th Anniversary Celebration

Knowing it was one of my favorite songs, Wayne and Alan sang *Time In A Bottle.* Wayne had prepared a trivia game with questions from the year 1967. For example, the average price of a house was $14,200; the price of gas was 32 cents a gallon.... This game was to determine which of the two of us was smarter. Our grandson Luke and great nephew, Sawyer, helped with the game. I won. (What did you expect?)

DJ had prepared a delightful power point presentation of family photos through the years. My heart smiled as I watched memories unfold: Holidays, vacations, anniversaries, our boys growing, welcoming daughters-in-law, each new grandchild, everyday life.... The joy of those memories also made my heart leak through my eyes as I brushed away grateful tears.

Alan and Wayne sang duets. Drake sang a song he said he had "writed" for us. He titled it *They Love*. To realize that our five-year-old grandson had witnessed what he knew to be love was a moment I will hold in my heart forever.

Christy, Margaret and Doyle made remarks about how David and I had touched their lives. They spoke of the joy of our love, emotions of pain we had known, celebrations we had enjoyed together. And into that mix, they sprinkled humor that brought laughter to everyone.

One of the most meaningful presentations was the sand ceremony. This ceremony originated years ago when a couple would bring sand from their birthplace and pour it into a vessel to represent the blending of their lives into one.

David and Martha ~ The Sand Ceremony

Ours represented the colors of our world. Each family member poured sand into a beautiful vase given to me by McKenna Stewart, granddaughter of Pastor David Warren.

As each family member poured sand into the lovely vessel, it became more beautiful. Colors built on each other just as every family member had added color to our world. Without having been instructed to do so, each of them gave us a hug after they poured the sand into the vase. Together Wayne and Ashley poured pink sand representing our precious new granddaughter expected to arrive in March 2018.

Sand Vase

Alan read a meaningful poem, "Bands of Gold." The verses celebrating a couple's 50th anniversary declared the gold was not in the ring but in the love, trust and hope they shared – a marriage carved in gold. Alan, touched by the poem, fought tears as he read it; and tears leaked from my eyes as I heard it.

To end our delightful celebration, Wayne asked the congregation to join the family in singing a song our sons had written to celebrate us, "I Choose You." It was meaningful and humorous (as our 50 years had been). The family passed out copies so guests could read the words. The memory of an entire congregation joining in – smiling faces, voices blending in song and laughter brought to mind another one of my favorite songs, "We Have This Moment."

Following a program that beautifully portrayed our love, we had a reception in the fellowship hall. Realizing that most people would have eaten lunch, we chose a light menu. The opulent presentation offered several choices. Family members served. To have Jenn here from California to serve as a hostess meant so much to me. Grace baked a small cake for cutting and 50 cupcakes. She spent hours perfecting them. Guests could hardly believe a 17-year-old had created such delicacies.

Celebration Cake and Cupcakes
Created by Grace Autumn Bass

The event began at 2:00 p.m. Sunday, the time we were wed 50 years ago, Sunday, December 31, 1967. Guests expressed how much they enjoyed it and said they would never forget it.

As guests were leaving, an unexpected ice storm had hit with a vengeance. It took people hours to get home. We lived four miles away; it took us an hour. We thanked God for keeping friends and family safe. There were no accidents en route home. For many, it meant a long drive.

The Bass Family ~ Those Happy Golden Years

11

Meditation: The Significance of Eight

As I mentioned on the day of my last infusion, my journey had been eight months long. Numbers have always been interesting to me.

- Number One signifies a new beginning.
- Number Two is associated with harmony, balance, consideration and love.
- Number Three signifies the Trinity as well as beginning, middle and the end.
- Number Four is the number of justice and stability that you need to keep in your life. It also resonates with loyalty, patience, wisdom and trust.
- Number Five represents divine grace.
- Number Six is considered a symbol of human weakness, sin and imperfection.
- Number Seven signifies completeness.

In my research, the revelation of the number eight gave me chills and thrills. It represents infinity and everything good in the universe which is infinite, such as infinite love, infinite supply, infinite time. In other words, eight signifies complete and unending abundance without any lack. Infinite is limitless or endless, impossible to measure or calculate. In the Bible, the number eight signifies resurrection and regeneration. It follows number seven, completeness plus one; and one is a new beginning.

On December 22, 2016 when I discovered a lump in my breast, there was no way I could have calculated or measured the journey on which it would lead me. I was about to embark upon the most frightening path I had ever traveled. But I had someone who would take the trip with me just as HE promised. Ephesians 3:20: *Now to Him who is able to do exceedingly abundantly above all that we ask or think, according to the power that works in us.* (NKJV)

After receiving the diagnosis, "You have cancer," I was shocked to numbness. There are no words to describe the devastation I felt in that moment. I had no choice, I had to accept it. Statistics show that one out of eight women will be diagnosed with breast cancer this year. I was one of eight.

Did I want to go through chemotherapy? NO! But every time I walked into the chemo lab, sat in the chair and saw other chairs filling up, I knew I was not alone. There were other dear ladies on that battlefield fighting for their lives just as I was. God's grace was abundant in helping me through 15 treatments and the devastating side effects that followed them.

David gave me a shirt that reads, "Sometimes God will put a Goliath in your life, for you to find the David within you." This man who has been my companion for nearly 50 years, knows exactly what I need just when I need it.

I've had bad hair days. But I did not want to lose my hair! In spite of the fact that I did, I was shown an abundance of love. When my hairdresser gave me the pixie haircut and shaved my head, she would not take a dime for her services. God sent a stranger to give me a $2 bill, a direct message from my dad in heaven to let me know I was going to be alright.

My twin had her hair cut short and got matching wigs for us to wear when we were together. A lady from our church, my sister-in-law, Katrinia, a "cancer sister," and the American Cancer Society also gave me a wig. I had an infinite supply of wigs that enabled me to be a gray-haired grandmother, a platinum blond, a feisty brunette or a bomb-shell red head. Furthermore, Katrinia knitted several caps so I could cover my bald head.

After I completed chemo treatments and my hair started to grow back, it was very curly. My "chemo curls" (as they are called) lasted only seven months. But during that time, I thanked God for my abundance of curls and enjoyed "my new look" on which I got many compliments.

As I said, I have always been a person who walked through life running. Chemo fatigue slowed me to a halt, giving me an abundance of time to rest. There were times when I woke to say, "That was the best movie I ever slept through." I had to study the Bible, read books on healing and inspiration that built my faith, words of encouragement and hope that helped me keep fighting. While there were times I found myself begging God to help me through the next minute, I also found time to thank Him for His infinite love, grace, mercy and comfort. On days when I had no energy to prepare a meal, David and I were amazed at the abundance of food that filled our freezer. Family, church family, coworkers, friends and neighbors brought so much food there were actually times we had to turn down offers as we had no place to put more.

When I started to feel anxious or depressed, there was an abundance of care, compassion, concern and thoughtfulness. At low ebbs, another stack of cards would arrive in the mail with words of hope and encouragement; emails came on a regular basis; my phone rang time and again. I read and heard, "I'm praying for you. I could not get you off my mind so I asked God to give you strength and peace.

Onzell Moore, a dear friend of my mom's, had taken the cancer journey before me. Knowing the additional pain of loss I bore with my Mother having left for heaven; this precious lady took me under her wings. Just when I thought I could not take another step; my phone would ring. Upon answering, I would hear her sweet voice, "You can make it. You can do this, Honey. The Lord will help you." She will never know what her love, empathy and compassion meant to me. God also sent written promises to me, confirming her encouragement, that I could read time and again, assuring me of His love:

John 14:27: Peace I leave with you, My peace I give to you; not as the world gives do I give to you. Let not your heart be troubled, neither let it be afraid. (NKJV)

Isaiah 41:13: For I, the LORD your God, will hold your right hand, Saying to you, 'Fear not, I will help you. (NKJV)

Due to the fact that I had triple negative breast cancer, I was told that for the next three years, I would need to be seen by an oncologist every three months. Each time I went for a follow-up visit, I was amazed and reminded of God's infinite goodness.

Mary Lambeth, a friend of mine, introduced me to a song that held a personal message for me. She will never know how many times it gave me courage to keep going. I sang it from my heart when I needed that reminder. It will continue to be part of my story, part of my healing. It goes hand in hand with my theme song: *I Know Who Holds Tomorrow.*

How Do I Know

Verse 1

My burden was heavy, my head was bowed low
I didn't know where to turn or which way to go
Then from a tree above me I heard a sparrow sing,
And I knew God was still in control of everything.

Chorus
How do I know? A little bird told me so.
And the lilies of the field joined the song.
They sang he takes care of these and we believe
He will take good care of you.
Verse 2
It is written in the Bible plain enough for all the see
By His riches in glory, He will meet all our needs.
If He cares for the lilies and sparrows that fall,
Why should I worry? He cares for me most of all.

Just as the little bird in the song told me, I am telling you. No matter what you face in life, when you can't see any good in it, God will be there loving you, strengthening you, giving you what you need to face the next day, hour and minute.

Romans 5:3-4: "And we rejoice in the hope of the glory of God, not only so, but we also rejoice in our sufferings, because we know that suffering produces perseverance, perseverance character, and character hope. And hope does not disappoint us, because God has poured out His love into our hearts by the Holy Spirit whom He has given us."

Each three-month appointment at Hope Cancer Center in 2018 gave me reason to be thankful. I was "cancer free."

In January 2019, a 3-D mammogram indicated that an ultrasound was necessary. In my left breast there appeared to be a problem. The news was momentarily devastating. Once again, I put on a brave mask but my head screamed, "No! No!" The biopsy and MRI revealed a diagnosis of DCIS (Ductal carcinoma insitu). The tumor appeared to be contained in the duct, which was good news. Options were another mastectomy or lumpectomy. After much prayer, I chose the latter. The simple procedure performed at Mission Hospital on March 1 proved to be my best choice! David and Alan accompanied me that day. Not long after we got home, DJ arrived.

Through the years, on the journey of Motherhood, I must have done something right. No one could have treated their mother with more love, care and respect than my three sons showed to me during the darkest chapter of my life.

Biopsies were sent to a more sophisticated lab; results came back that this was not even cancer but hyperplasia, pre-cancer. This problem was caught early, enabling me to avoid another trip down "cancer lane!" No follow-up treatment was necessary. So many prayers were going up to God on my behalf. And again, He heard and answered them!

Epilogue

In my narrative, you read that David and I traveled from the mountains to the beach. Asheville had been our home for 46 years. The commute was becoming arduous. We were going back and forth to keep up maintence on both home sites. Realizing we were not getting younger, we started talking about settling in one place. The decision was not a quick one. We had strong ties in both places. After much prayer and many debates, we made the choice to put the round house on the market and settle in Southport. Thus began the process for the big move. Believe me, after 38 years in one house, it was a big one!

Round house in Asheville

Several factors came into play. Ron and Margaret own a place two doors down from ours in Southport and will be coming as often as possible. Their visits are bright spots.

Knowing we don't have to head back to Asheville every week or so is a blessing. Doyle and several members of David's family live in Fayetteville, two hours away. We will have opportunities to spend more time with them as well.

David and I have owned a place on Oak Island or in Southport since 1986 and love the area. In 1998 we bought a double-wide on Jib Street and in 2014, replaced it with a four-bedroom manufactured home, two miles from the coast. We enjoy walks on the beach and the awesome Oak Island sunsets. What a way to settle in for retirement!

The decision to call Southport home was one of the best we ever made. Our neighbors welcomed us with open arms:

- Mickey and Kathy Embler, who enjoy canning vegetables and fruits often bring us canned goods and fresh vegetables. Underneath a bed in one of our guest rooms has become my storage bin. On many days, these friends prepare hot meals and call for me to come "pick up something."
- Buddy and Joyce Thomas often share baked goods right out of the oven and vegetables from their garden. One day Joyce painted her mailbox post and while she was at it, decided to paint ours, too.
- Mark and Ami Briggs share fresh collards from their garden and fresh jellies they have canned. For years, this kind neighbor picked up our mail and kept it for us until we returned.
- Carmela Gonka, Kathy Williams and Sandy Cagle, my walking buddies from the neighborhood in back of ours, passed by when I was outside and invited me to join them. Those gals make any day a brighter one on our walks.

That's the simple lifestyle here; it's how folks live. Life doesn't get much better than that.

My medical records have been transferred from Hope Cancer Center in Asheville to Cape Fear Cancer Specialty in Wilmington. My January 2020 3-D mammogram at this site was clear (cancer-free) with my next one scheduled for January 2021. Those tests are done annually now.

I will continue to see Dr. Caldwell from time to time to keep in touch with the kind physician who has become a forever friend. He recommended that I find a local doctor but told me he would see me whenever I needed him. At the recommendation of the Emblers, I have seen a local doctor with whom I feel totally comfortable. She encouraged me to continue to see Dr. Caldwell and assured me she would be here for me when I needed her.

Watching life fall into place is one confirmation after the other that we are "home where we belong." We enjoy having family and friends visit us. They clearly see why we love our Southport Haven.

Retirement home in Southport

On July 31, 2017, the news that Wayne and Ashley were expecting a child gave me added hope to fight hard and win my cancer battle. It kept me going on days when I did not think I could.

Charley Layne Bass arrived on March 13, 2018. David and I were in Bloomington the next day to meet her. As I held this bundle of love in my arms for the first time and looked into her angelic face, it was as though heaven and earth kissed. I felt it all the way to my heart. When I looked at my son Wayne, I realized this was not only a moment of hope and healing for me, it was also one for him. His prayer and ours that someday he would be a dad had been answered. As my eyes met his, there were no words. The look on his face said it all.

Meeting Charley Layne Bass
(A picture worth a 1,000 words)

Alan has moved to Hendersonville, North Carolina, purchased a lovely home and works online as an author for Wiley Publishers. We get together with him and Drake as often as possible. They enjoy coming back to Southport and we arrange follow-up doctor visits in Asheville to include overnight stays with them. Our endearing Drake is eight years old, growing up too fast, becoming dearer with every year. The compassion and love two of my heroes showed to me during my most difficult chapter of life is hard to put into words.

Alan and Drake

Our K-town family are enjoying their new home. DJ and Jamie stay busy in their jobs but as they always have, they still take time to make life special for each other and their children. Grace, our dear "first grand," is a sophomore at the University of Tennessee in Knoxville. She is a beautiful loving 20-year-old with high ambitions to do something meaningful with her life, pursuing a double major in math and English. Our mild-mannered and compassionate 17-year-old John, is a high school senior, already driving. He has earned his black belt in Krav Maga and enjoys back country camping. Our spirited, funny and talented Luke is a technical guru. A 14-year-old high school sophomore, he just built his own computer. He also enjoys back country camping.

We are proud of all of them and the young adults they are becoming. Our son, daughter-in-love and these three grands were so thoughtful during my "C" journey. The love they showed me was exceptional – inspiring in today's world. If it's possible, they are even more excited than we are about our living at the beach.

DJ, Jamie, Grace, John and Luke
(Our K-town Family)

Our Bloomington family are enjoying life in Illinois. This dear son and daughter-in-love were with me from the beginning when I got the dreadful "C" diagnosis and walked with me to the end of the journey. Day after day, I felt their love across the miles.

Wayne enjoys his role as a Professor of Humanities at Heartland Community College. Ashley works online for VetStem Biopharma and attends occasional out-of-town conferences.

Wayne, Ashley and Charley

We have been privileged to make the drive several times and enjoy our visits with them, honored to help Wayne while Ashley was out of town for her job. We have also enjoyed endless moments on Face Time. The precious two-year-old Princess Charley begs to "Face time with Grandma and Grandpa" and is ready to perform for us in whatever she is doing.

Time flies so quickly, like sand slipping through an hourglass. In July 2020, our entire family enjoyed another awesome Southport vacation. Through the years, I have wanted to hold memories tightly in my hand. I can't do that; but I will hold them in my heart forever.

There are too many blessings to count in this new life – this "new normal." As I face each new day, I thank God for it. I cherish it, knowing it is my present from Him. In these changing days still filled with questions and uncertainties, my theme song will continue to be *I Know Who Holds Tomorrow.*

After David and I moved to Southport, while going through some things, I found a quote in one of the many books or pamphlets I had read during my cancer journey. I don't know who wrote it; but it meant so much to me – summed up my journey so well – I wanted to share it with you.

A Thought From a Survivor

I have accepted cancer's presence in my life. I admit I have been changed inside and out. I believe I am more thoughtful and less quick to judge. I have discovered patience and fortitude within me that I otherwise may have never found. I have met incredible people connected to the cancer world. Perhaps it is my nature, but I admit there is a silver lining to cancer. Sometimes there are genuine golden gems that shine as caregivers and friends. If not for cancer, would I have recognized the goodness in others? - GSB

Writing my story has not been easy. As I reviewed the journal I had kept, added new notes and focused on particulars, at times I had to lay the manuscript aside. Remembering them was painfully overwhelming. But it was my desire to share details of this journey in a book, hoping my story would inspire anyone taking an arduous trek of any kind to press on and not give up.

I have been privileged to share my story in public settings. At Emma Church, I spoke on a Sunday morning. In March 2018, I was a featured speaker at Praise Temple Fellowship in Dallas, North Carolina. Mary Lambeth, the dear friend who introduced me to the little bird song, planned the event, "My Story Isn't Over Yet." My story of survival was included among five other women who spoke on other topics women face today: Abuse, Caregiving and Grief. Sharing our pain brings strength to others who have walked a similar journey, building faith and courage.

In August 2018, I was privileged to speak in a similar setting at Pecks Mill United Methodist Church in West Virginia. My friend, Kim Neil, organized the event with the same theme, "My Story Isn't Over Yet." Along with my story of survival, three other ladies spoke on Abuse, Grief and Brokenness. Ladies attending that conference drank our words in, realizing that their own stories held similar pain. Every woman has a story. Only the places and faces change the facts.

There were other opportunities to speak on my calendar in 2020. They had to be cancelled due to the COVID19 crisis with assurance that once restrictions had been lifted, I would be rescheduled to come and speak.

Whatever struggle you may be facing, be assured that nothing is too complicated for God. He promised never to leave or forsake you.

My battle was a journey through cancer. As you have read, it was not an easy one. But I survived and you can, too!

If my goal inspires or encourages any reader not to give up, then this venture was not in vain.

Cheering you on,

Martha Sue Wood Bass

Made in the USA
Monee, IL
08 November 2020